Elise

DISGUSTING CRITTERS

A CREEPY CRAWLY COLLECTION

HOWDY!

OH, HI!

HELLO!

tundra

For Marie, my little silkworm,
Sophie, my little fruit fly,
and Emma, who, like the spider, is not an insect

This edition published by Tundra Books, 2024

Tundra Books, an imprint of Tundra Book Group, a division of Penguin Random House of Canada Limited

Library and Archives Canada Cataloguing in Publication

Title: Disgusting critters : a creepy crawly collection / Elise Gravel.
Other titles: Works. Selections. English
Names: Gravel, Elise, author, illustrator. | Container of (expression): Gravel, Elise. Mouche.
  English. | Container of (expression): Gravel, Elise. Ver. English. | Container of (expression):
  Gravel, Elise. Araignée. English.
Description: A collection of three titles from Elise Gravel's Disgusting critters series. |
  Includes translations of: La mouche, Le ver, and L'araignée.
Identifiers: Canadiana 20230513727 | ISBN 9781774885796 (softcover)
Subjects: LCSH: Flies—Juvenile literature. | LCSH: Worms—Juvenile literature. | LCSH: Spiders—
  Juvenile literature. | LCGFT: Instructional and educational works. | LCGFT: Illustrated works.
Classification: LCC QL467.2 .G722 2024 | DDC j565/.7—dc23

Published simultaneously in the United States of America by Tundra Books of Northern New York, an imprint of Tundra Book Group, a division of Penguin Random House of Canada Limited

Library of Congress Control Number: 2023944175

Edited by Samantha Swenson
Designed by Elise Gravel and Gigi Lau
The artwork in this book was rendered digitally.
The text was set in Providence Sans Pro.

Printed in China

www.penguinrandomhouse.ca

1 2 3 4 5   28 27 26 25 24

Penguin
Random House
tundra   TUNDRA BOOKS

THE WORM

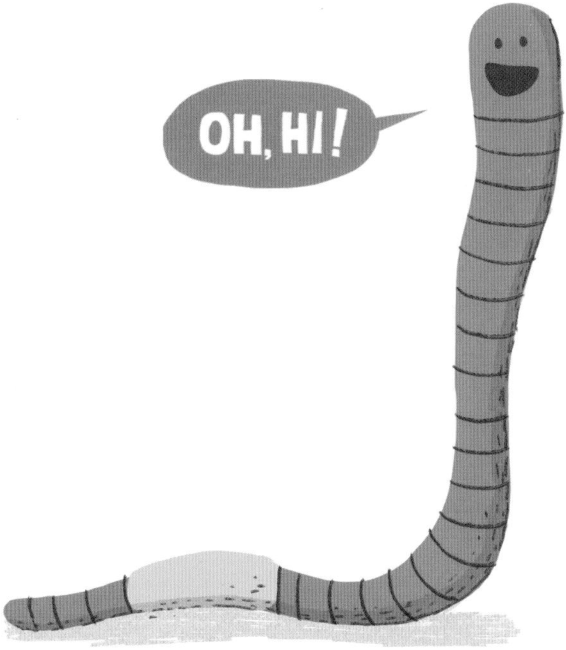
OH, HI!

LADIES AND GENTLEMEN,
I present to you

THE WORM.

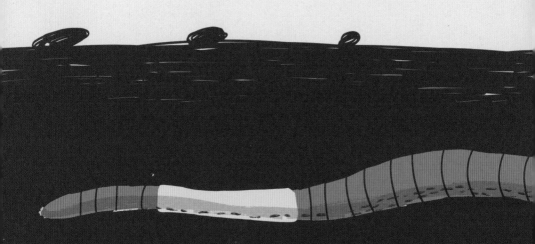

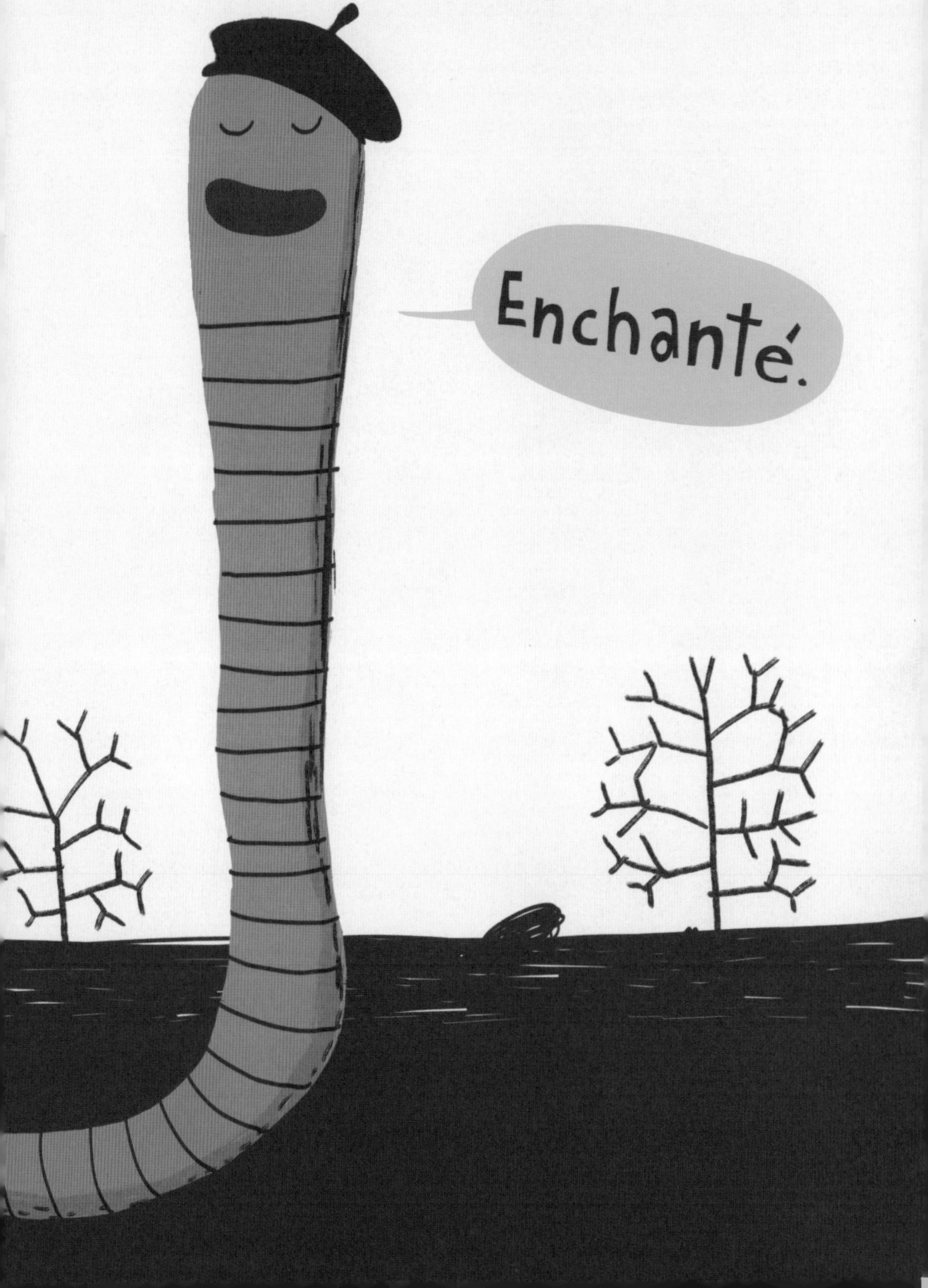
Enchanté.

The worm is a long animal that's shaped like a tube. It doesn't have a

SKELETON

or a spine: it's an

INVERTEBRATE.

It also doesn't have any legs.

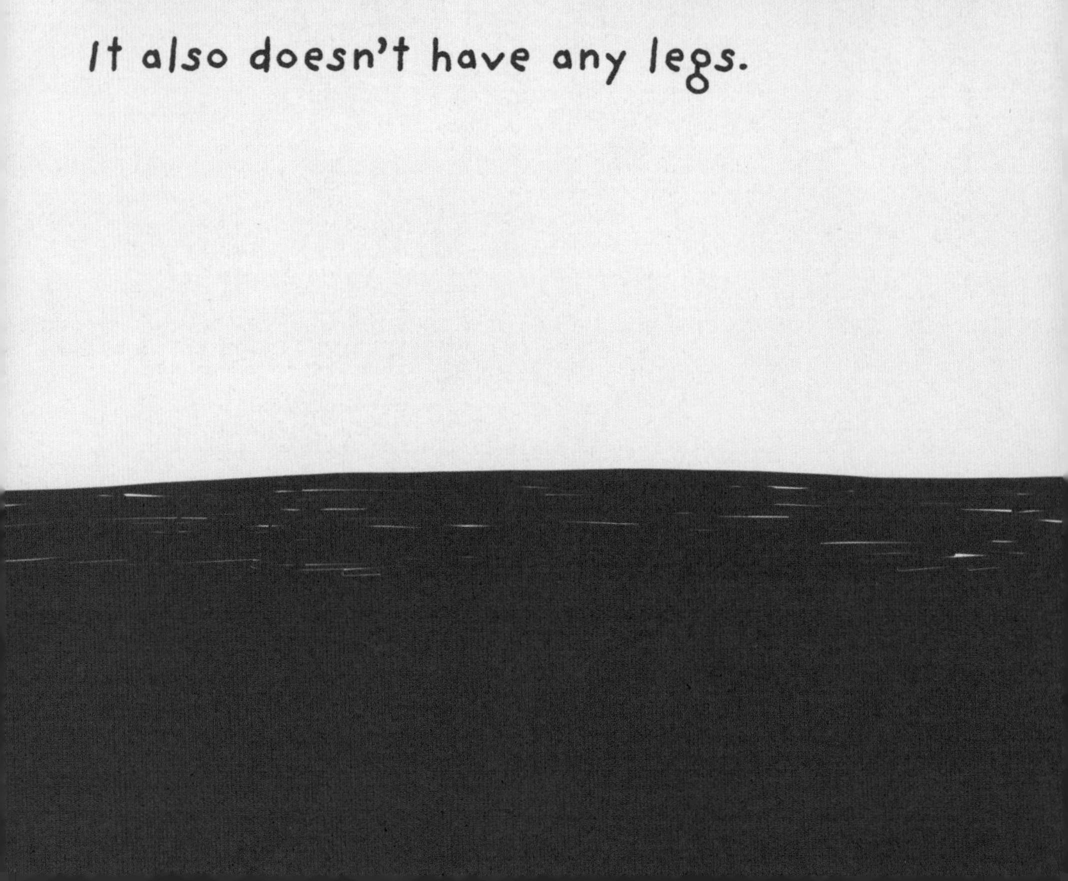

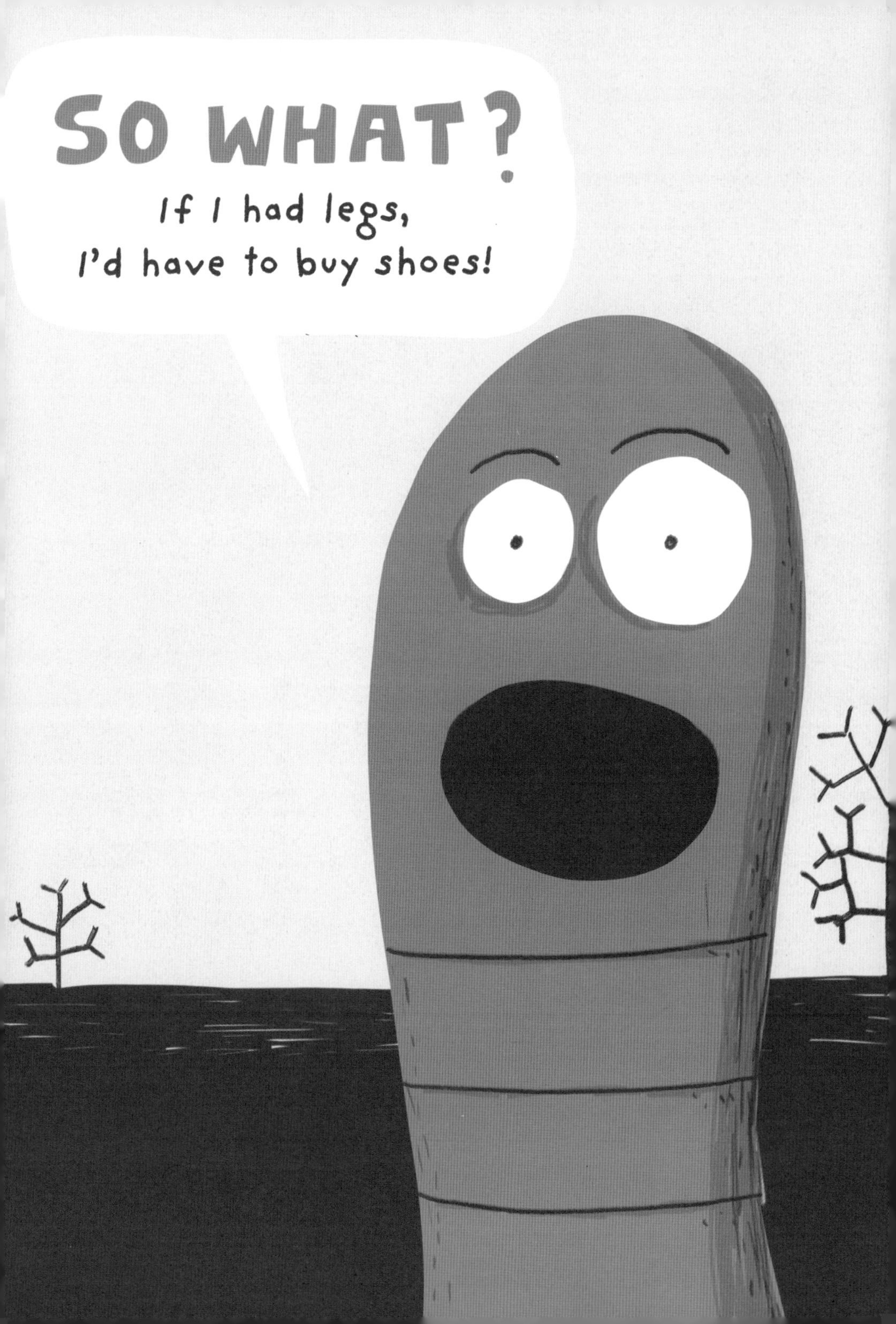
SO WHAT? If I had legs, I'd have to buy shoes!

There are many

DIFFERENT

kinds of worms.

HERE ARE SOME OF THEM:

THE EARTHWORM

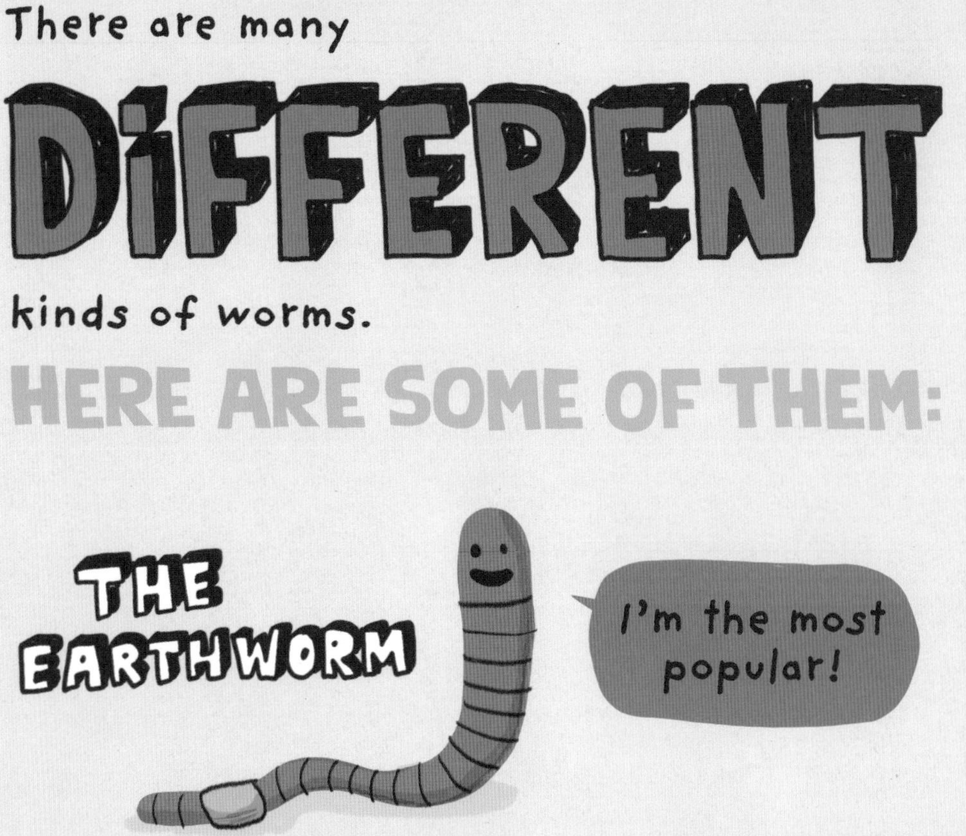
I'm the most popular!

THE TAPEWORM

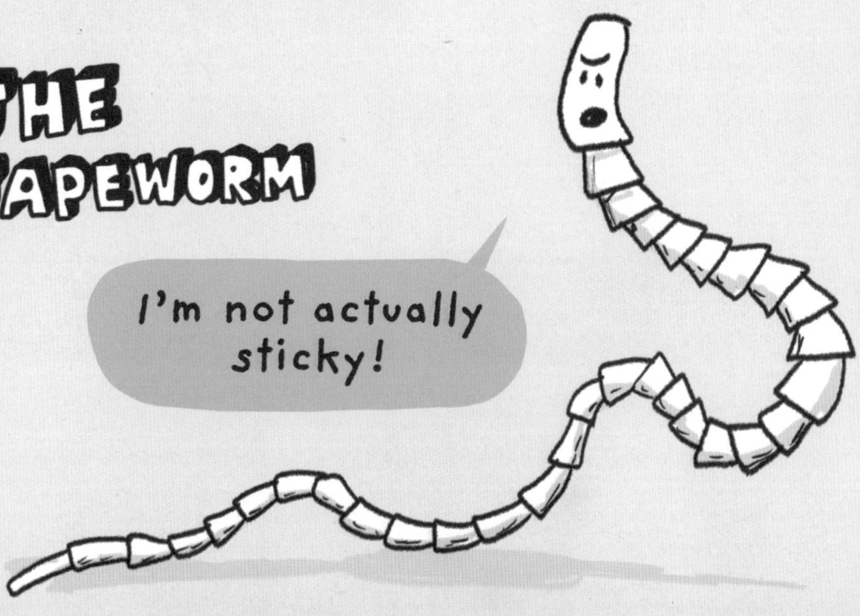
I'm not actually sticky!

THE FLATWORM

THE WHITE WORM

I'm called a worm, but I have legs!

Many insect larvae, like

THE MAGGOT

(baby fly)

Some worms are so small that you need a microscope to see them. Others can be 115 feet (35 meters) long, like the ribbon worm that lives in oceans and rivers.

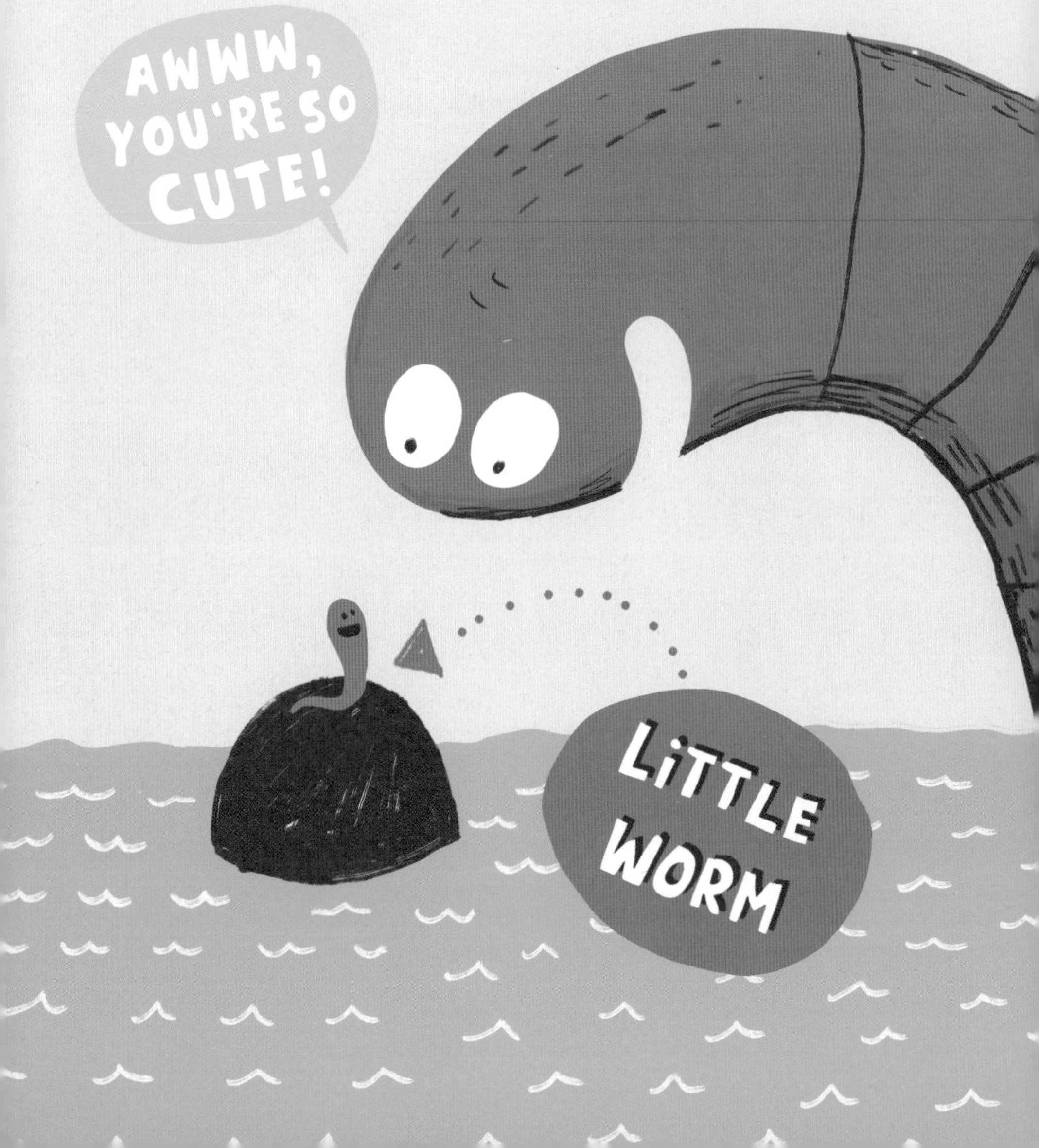
AWWW, YOU'RE SO CUTE!
LITTLE WORM

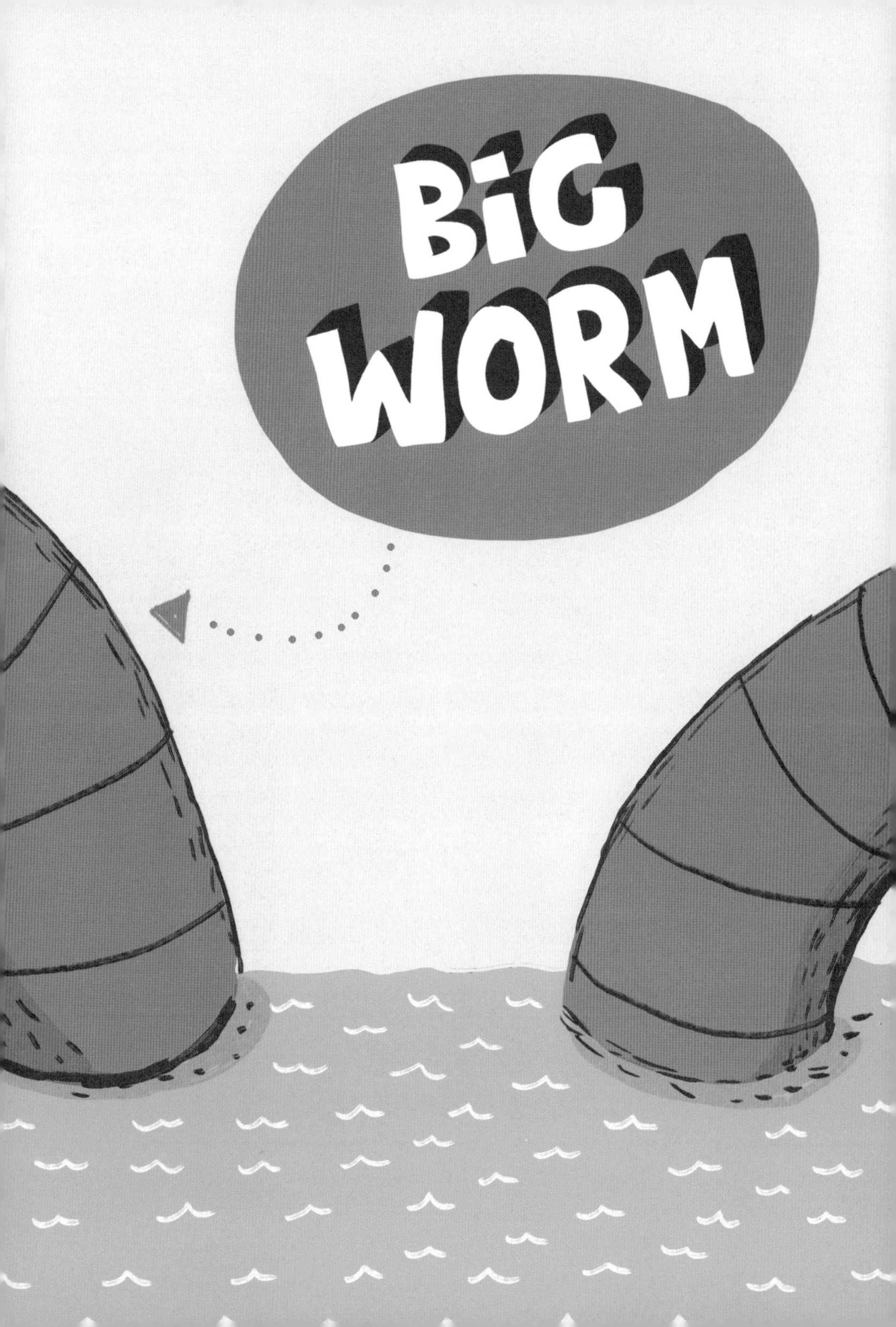
BIG WORM

Worms can live in different

HABITATS.

Some live in the water. Others live in rotting plants. Some even live inside human or animal bodies!

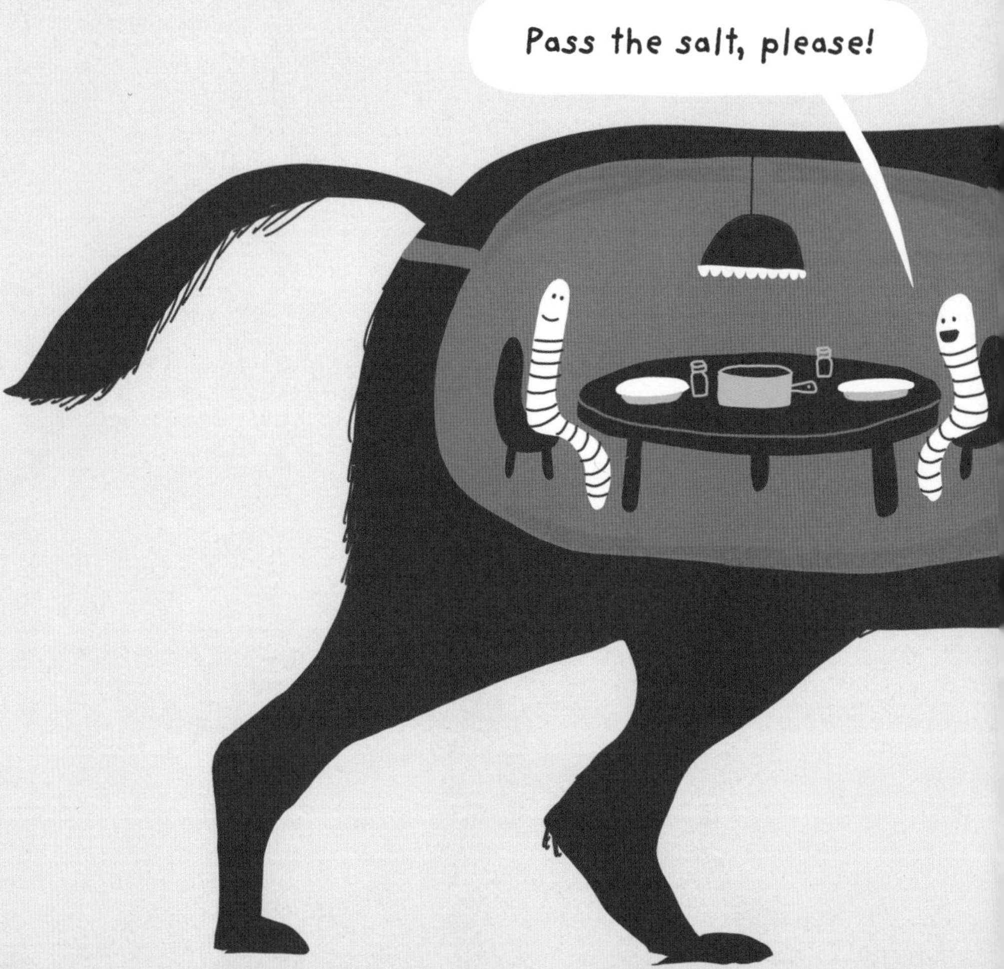
Pass the salt, please!

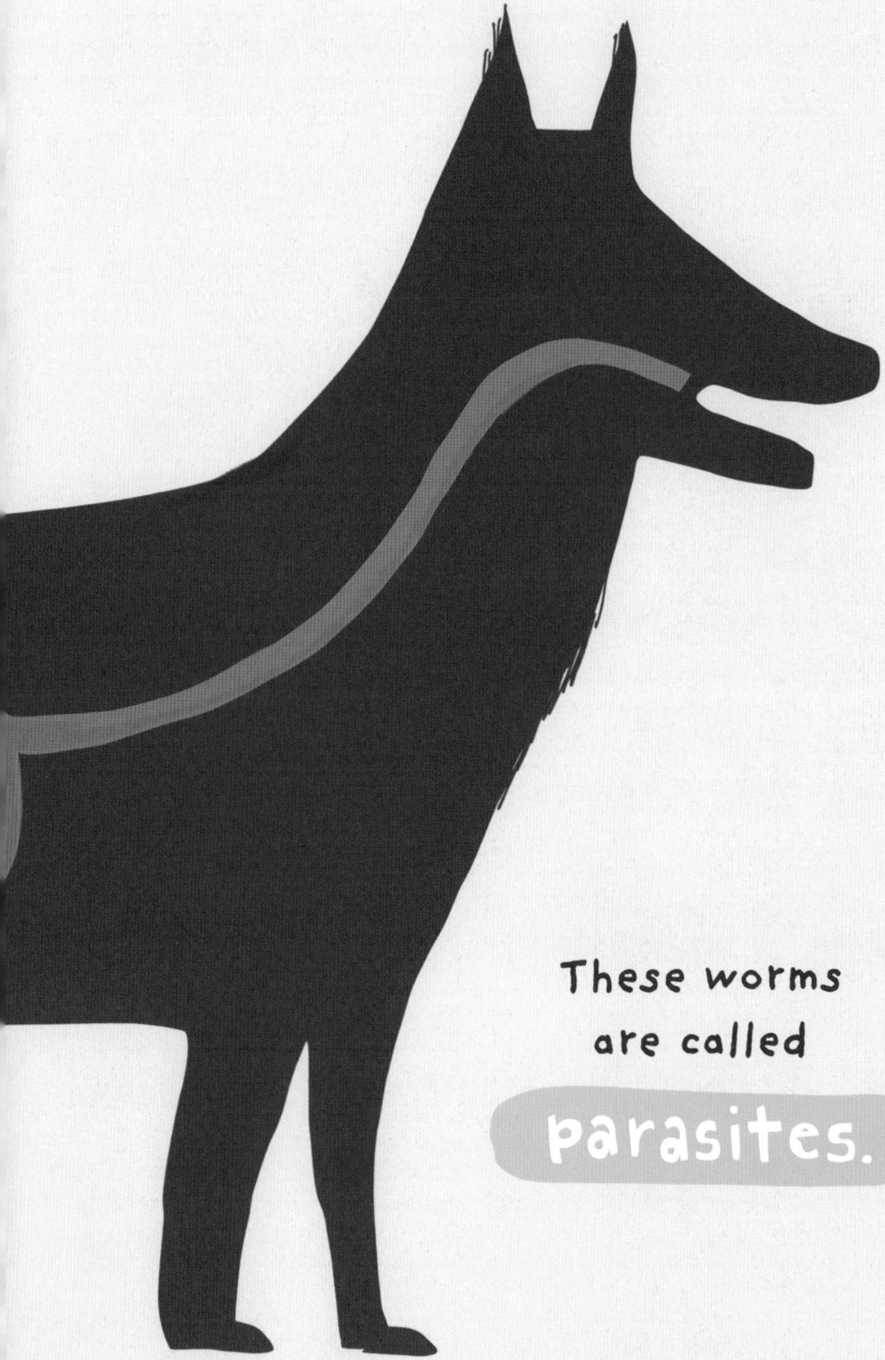

These worms
are called
parasites.

The most common worm is the

EARTHWORM.

An earthworm is basically a long

DIGESTIVE TRACT

inside a

MUSCLE TUBE.

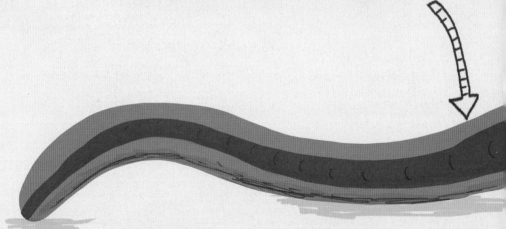

It's that muscle tube that's slimy and disgusting.

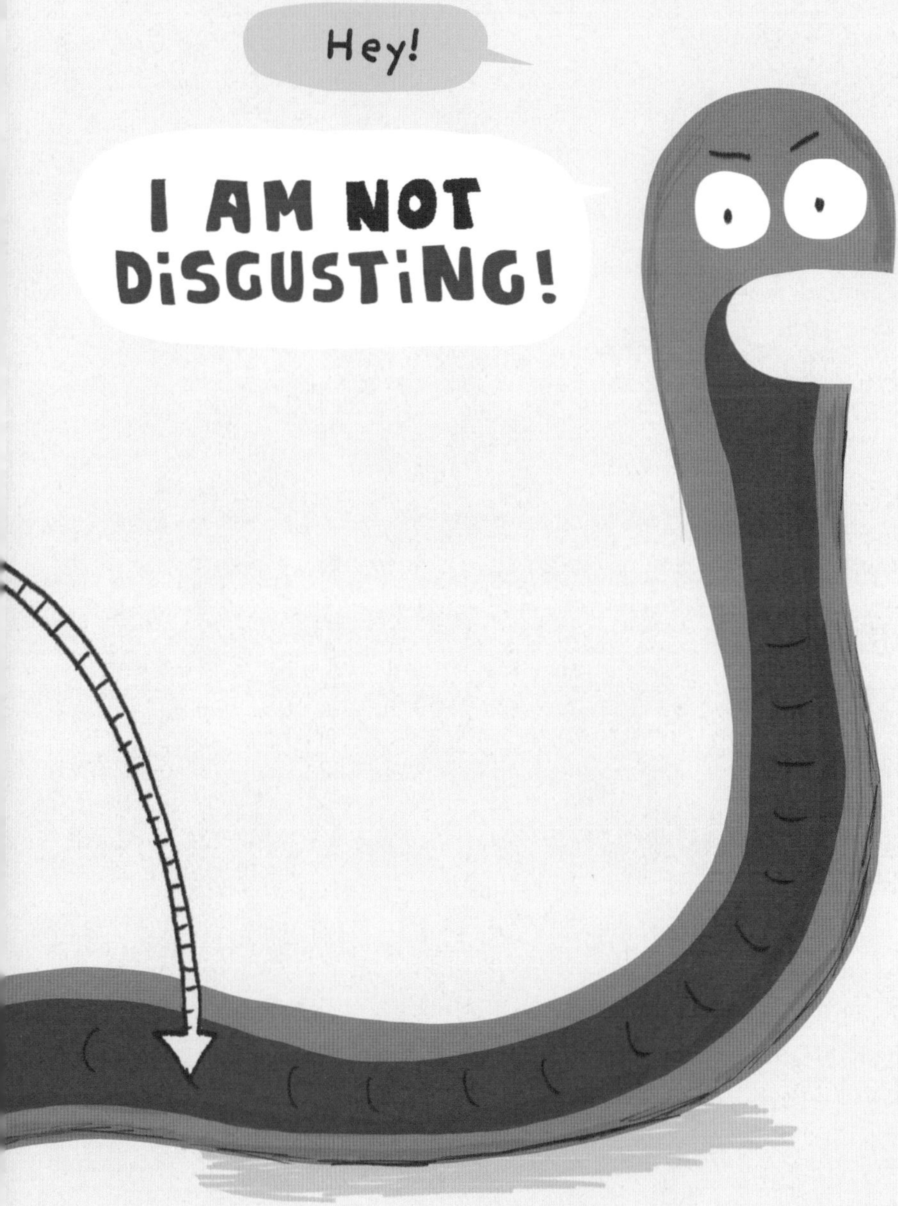

Worms have been on earth for

MiLLiONS OF YEARS!

Maybe even billions!

Biologists believe they evolved
with the

DiNOSAURS.

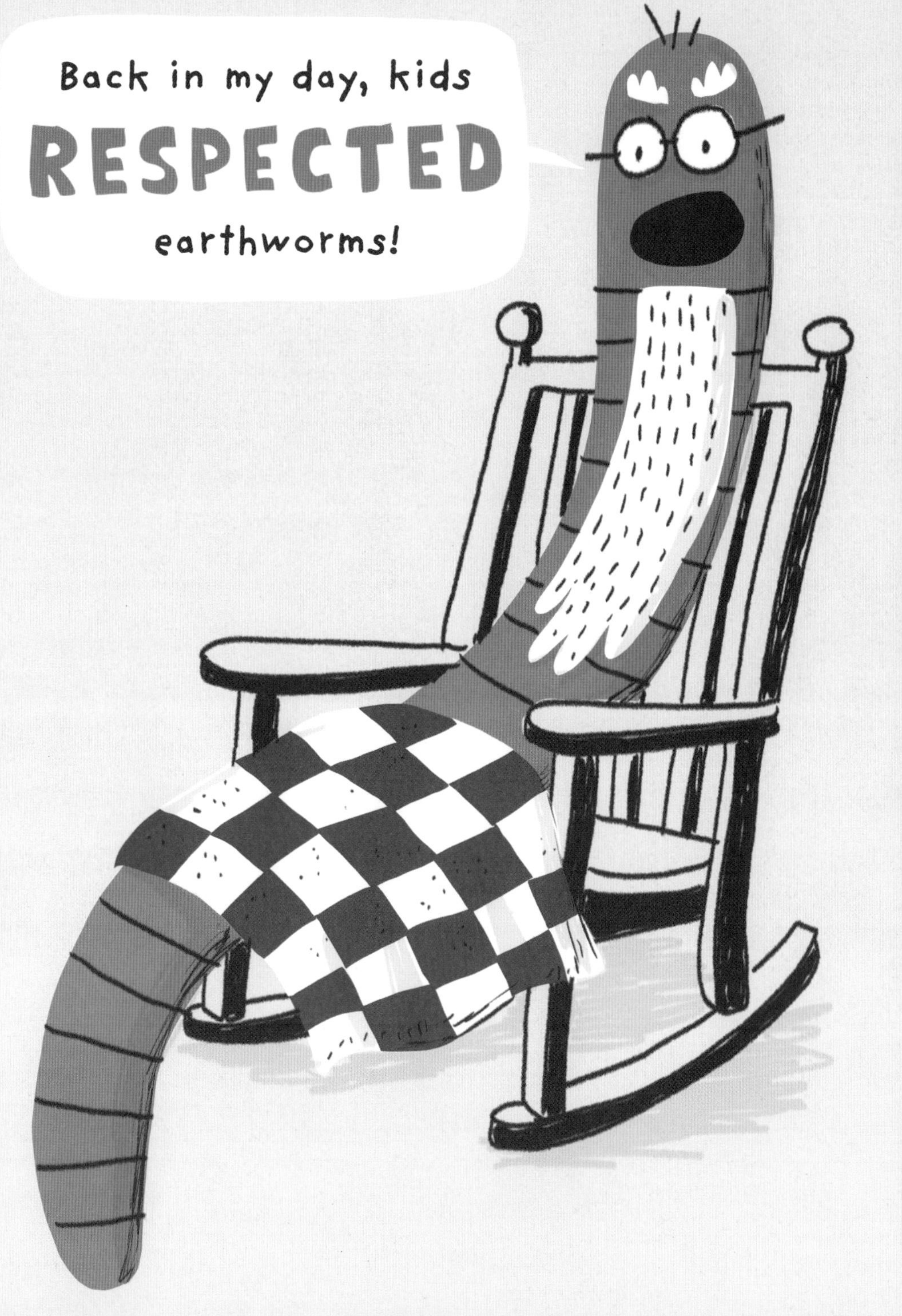
Back in my day, kids RESPECTED earthworms!

Earthworms have

NO EYES,

but they can sense light with
something called

PHOTORECEPTORS:

sensors in the worm's skin
that react to light.

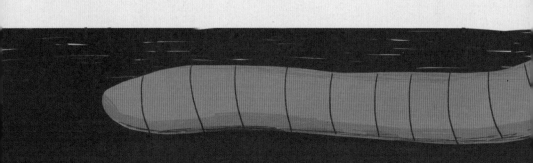

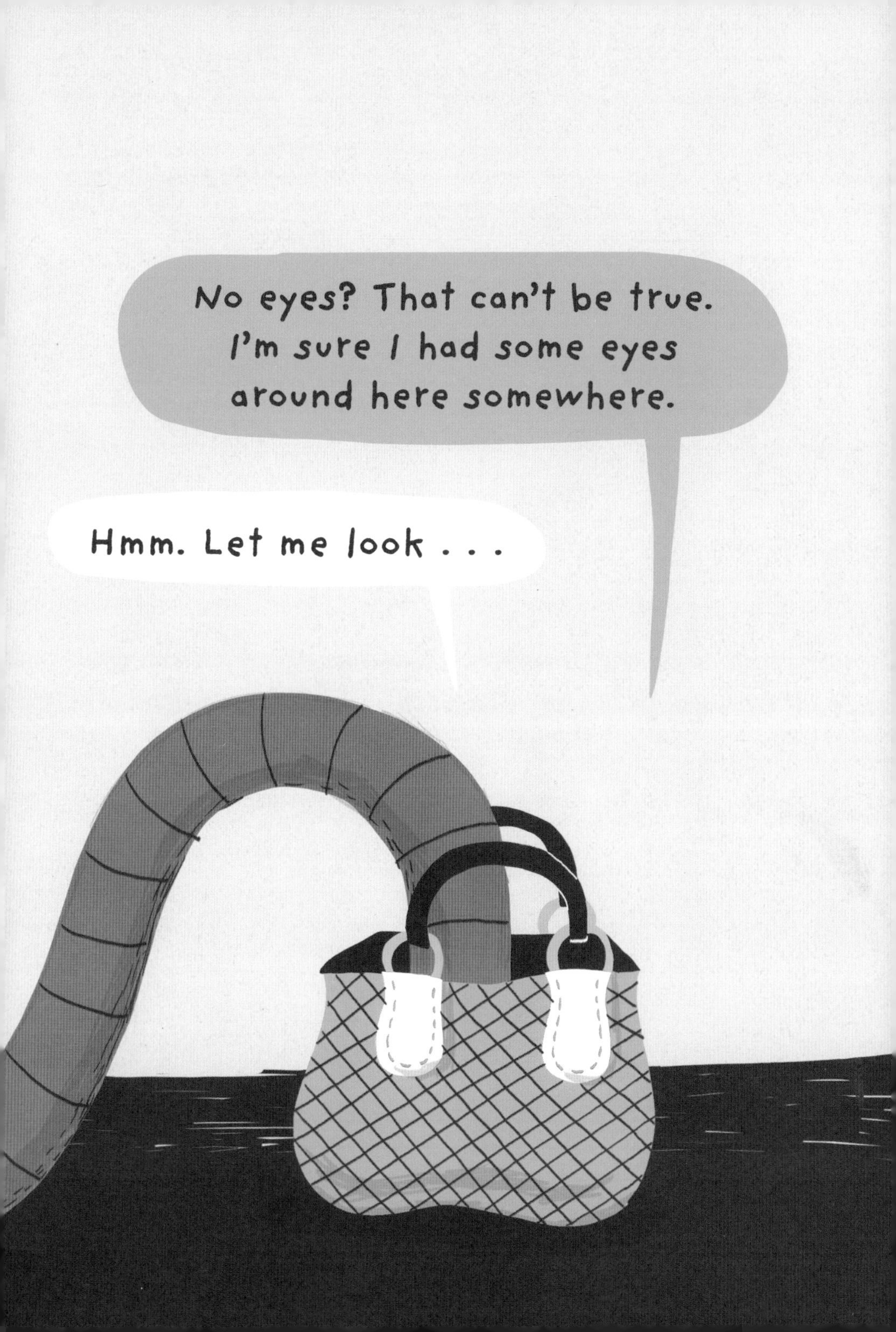
No eyes? That can't be true. I'm sure I had some eyes around here somewhere.
Hmm. Let me look . . .

Earthworms move by

SQUEEZING

their

MUSCLES,

causing their bodies to contract and expand.

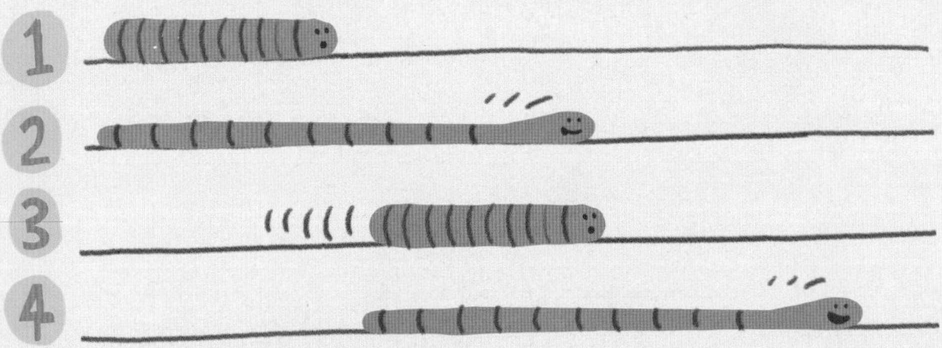
1
2
3
4

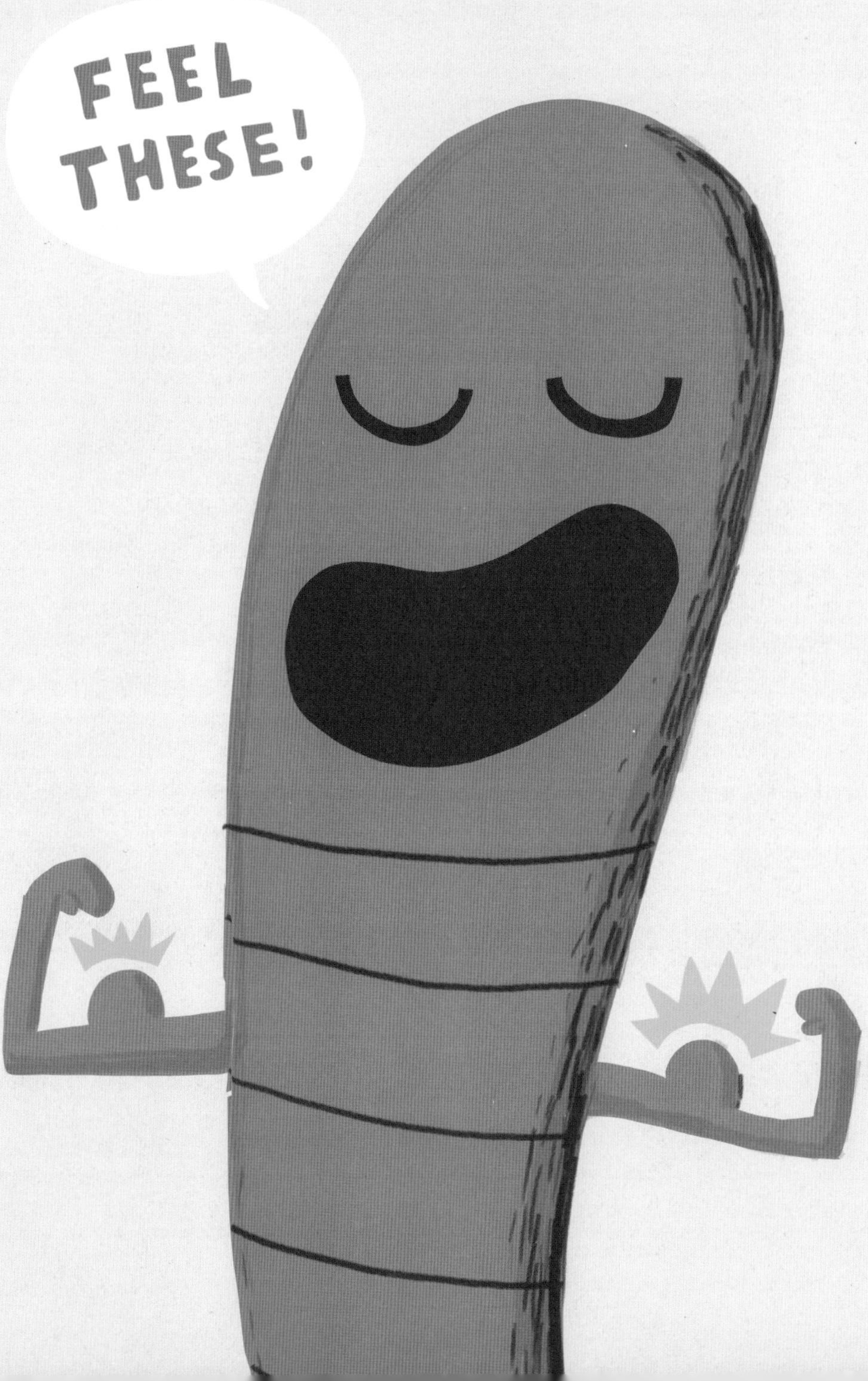
FEEL THESE!

Earthworms eat rotting plants and enrich the soil by making paths that let air and water circulate in it.

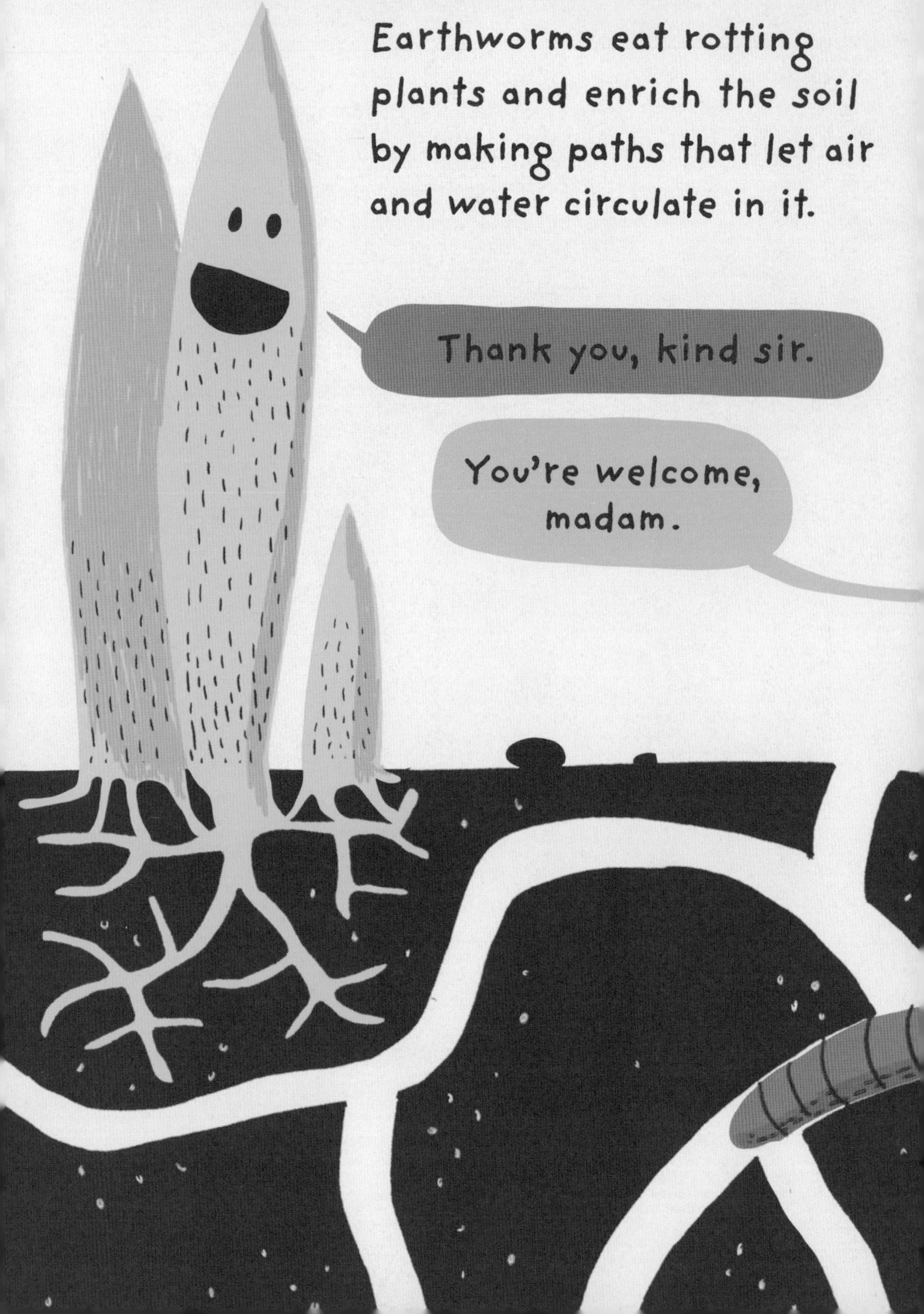
Thank you, kind sir.
You're welcome, madam.

IT'S GOOD for NATURE!

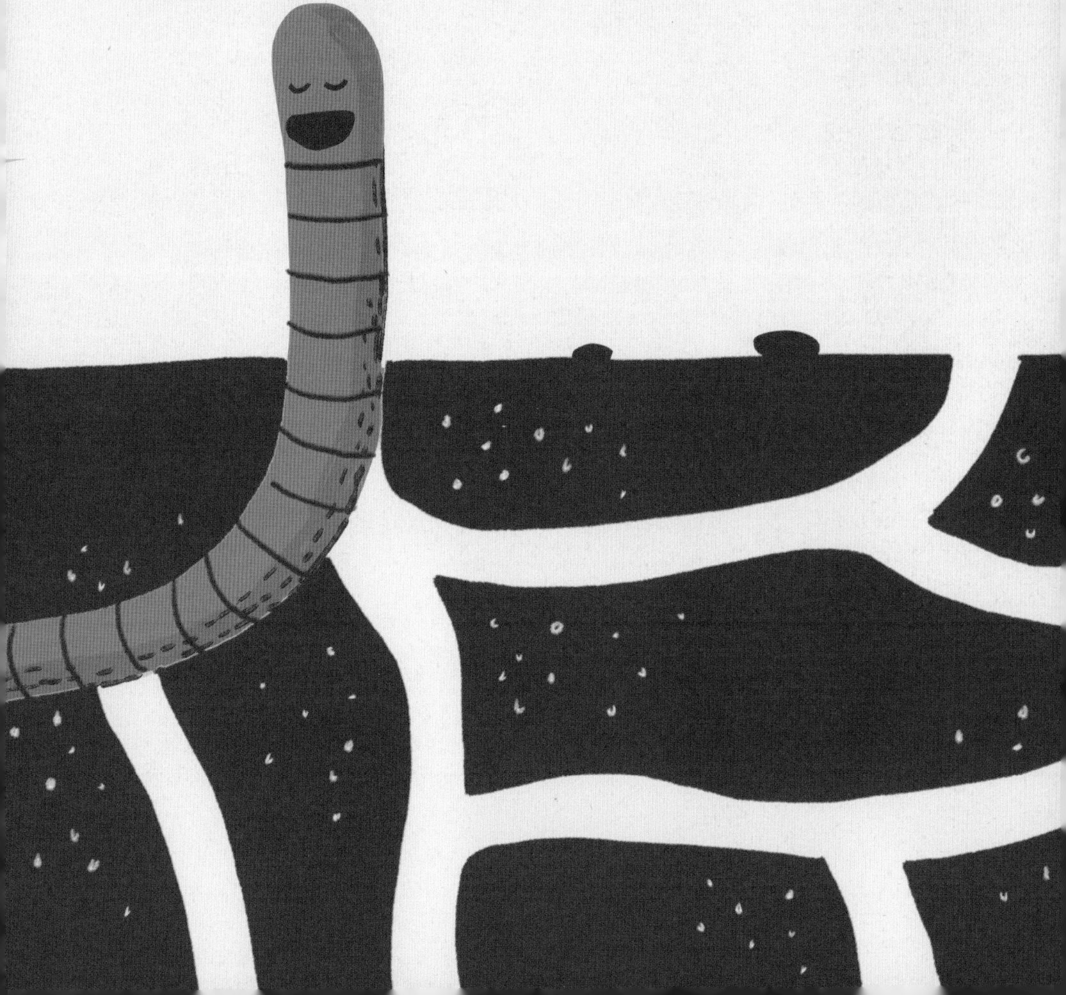

Many kinds of worms are hermaphrodites, which means they have both

MALE

and

FEMALE

reproductive organs.

In other words, an earthworm is a boy and a girl at the same time. They still need a partner to reproduce, though.

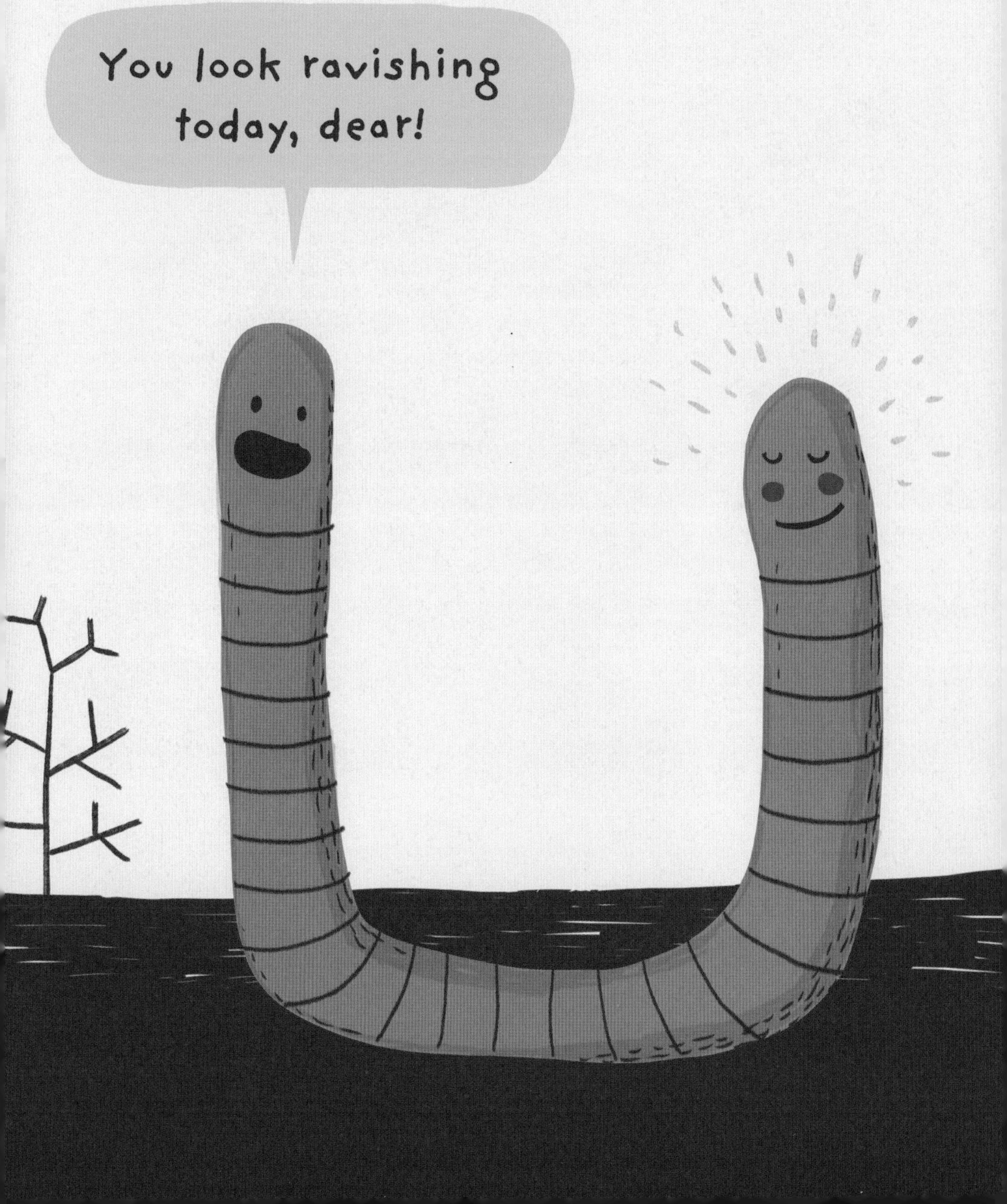
You look ravishing today, dear!

Earthworms might seem

PRETTY GROSS,

but they're very useful! They recycle nature's waste and help turn it into soil. Farmers and gardeners love earthworms!

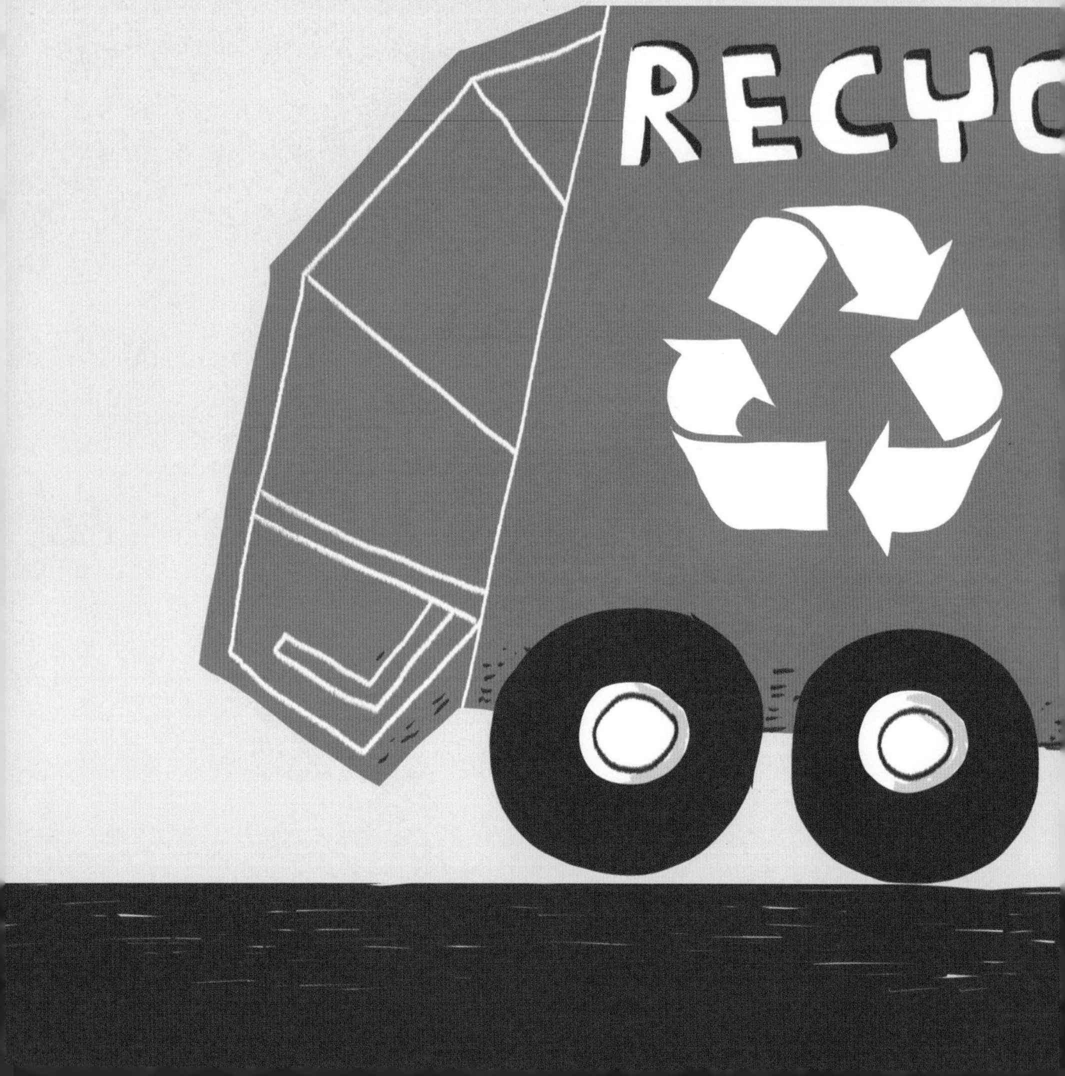
RECYC

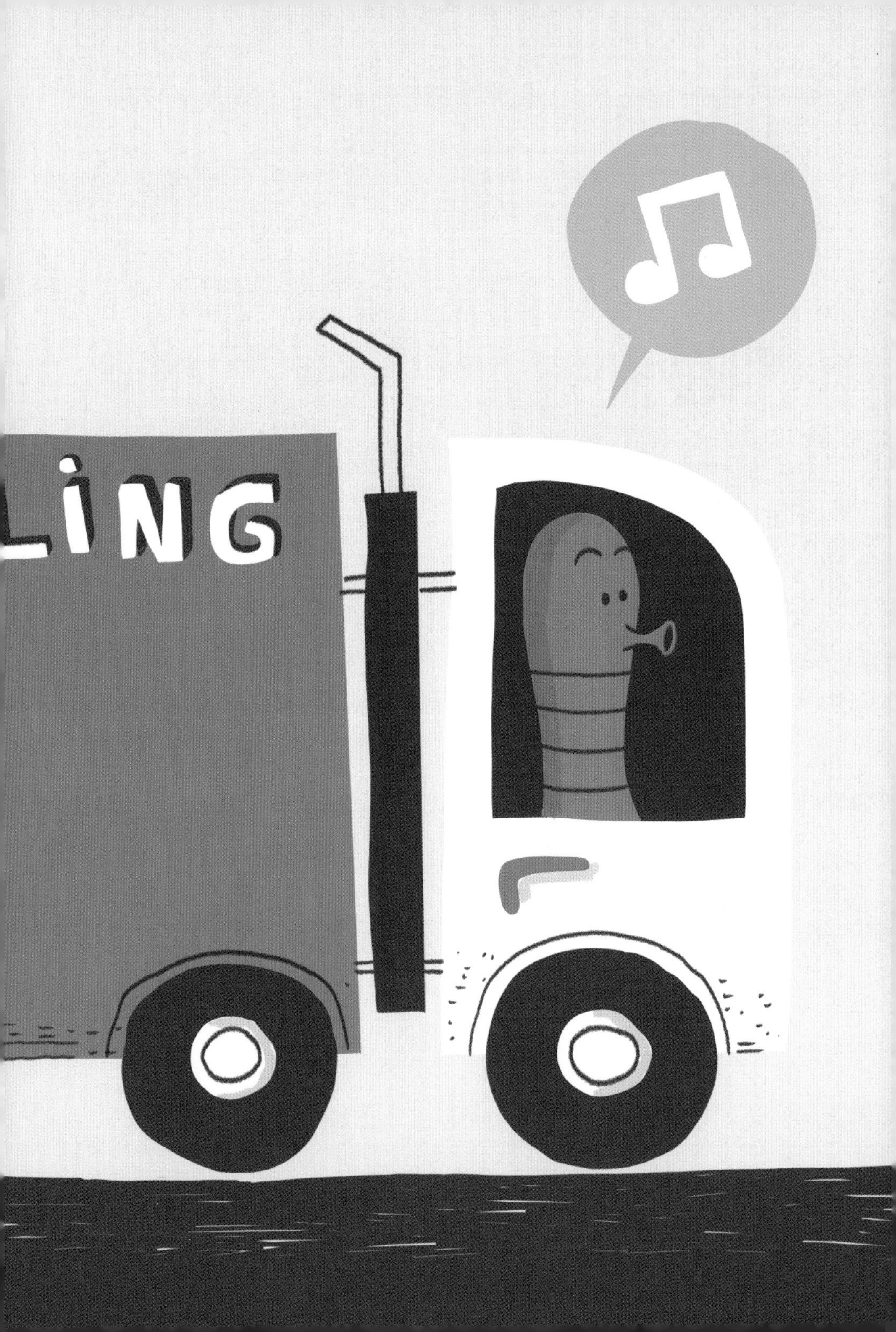
LING

Fishermen use earthworms to catch fish, and some people even eat them and find them

DELICIOUS!

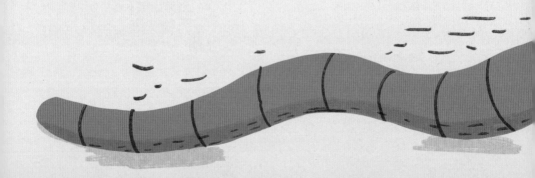

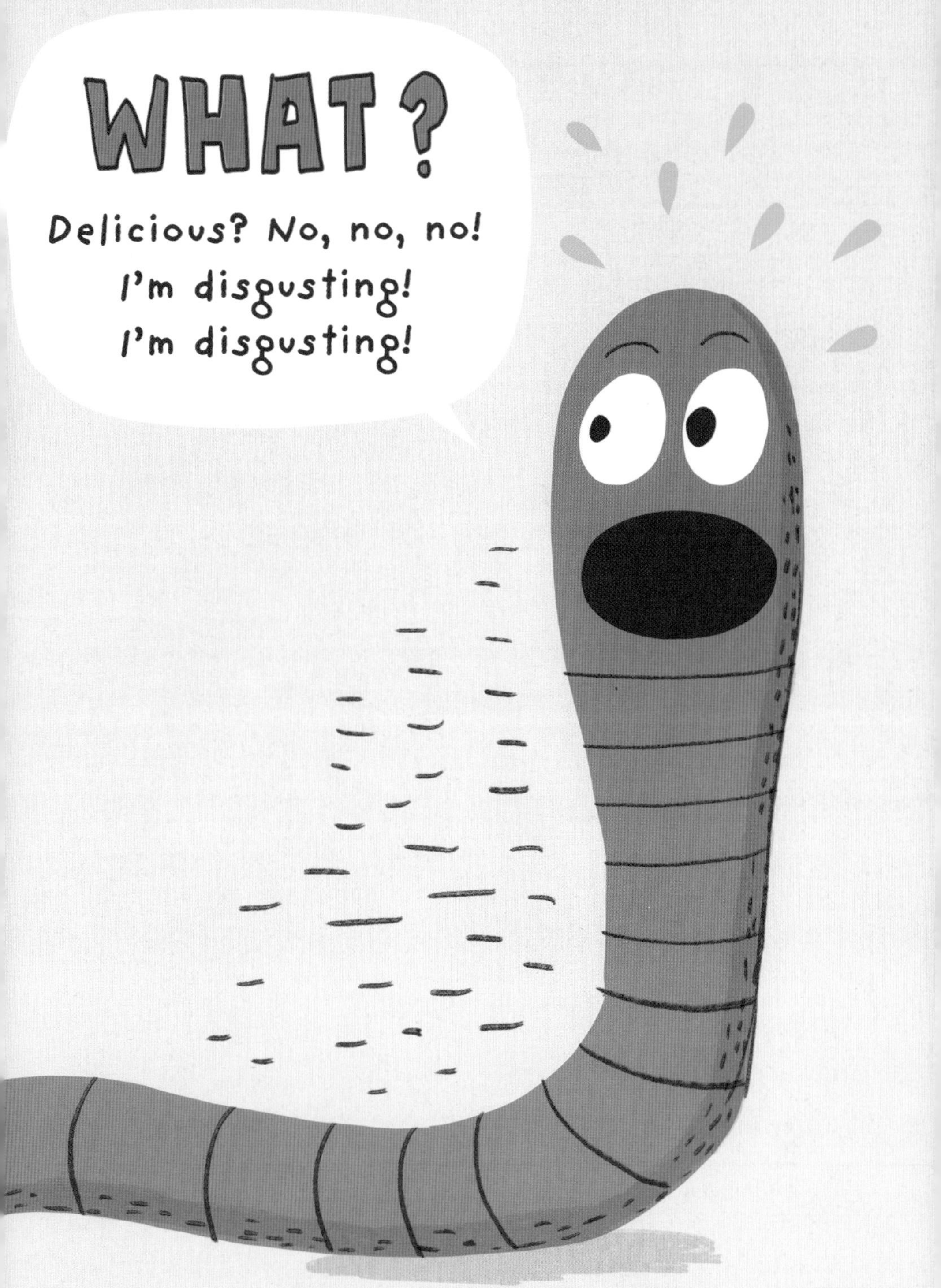
WHAT?
Delicious? No, no, no!
I'm disgusting!
I'm disgusting!

So next time you meet an earthworm, be polite. Worms are

YOUR FRIENDS!

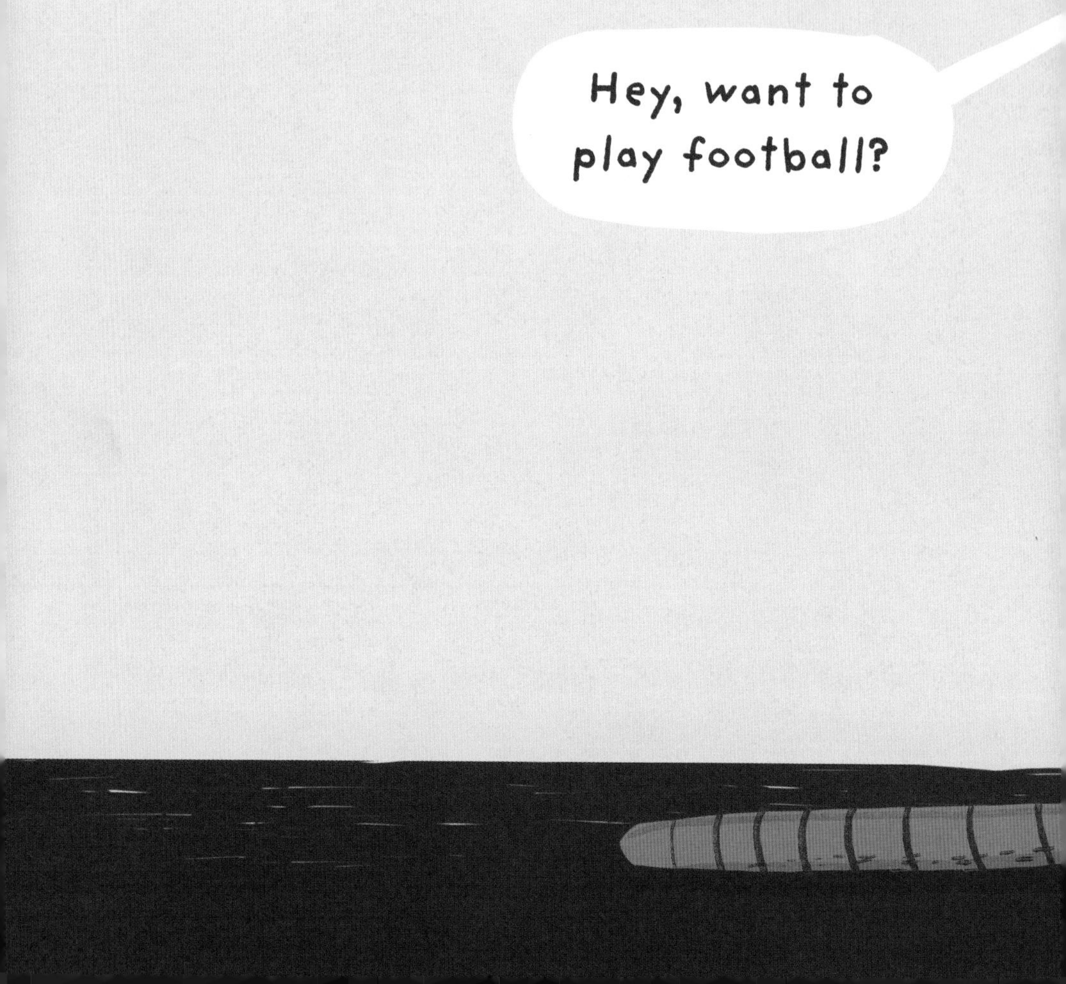
Hey, want to play football?

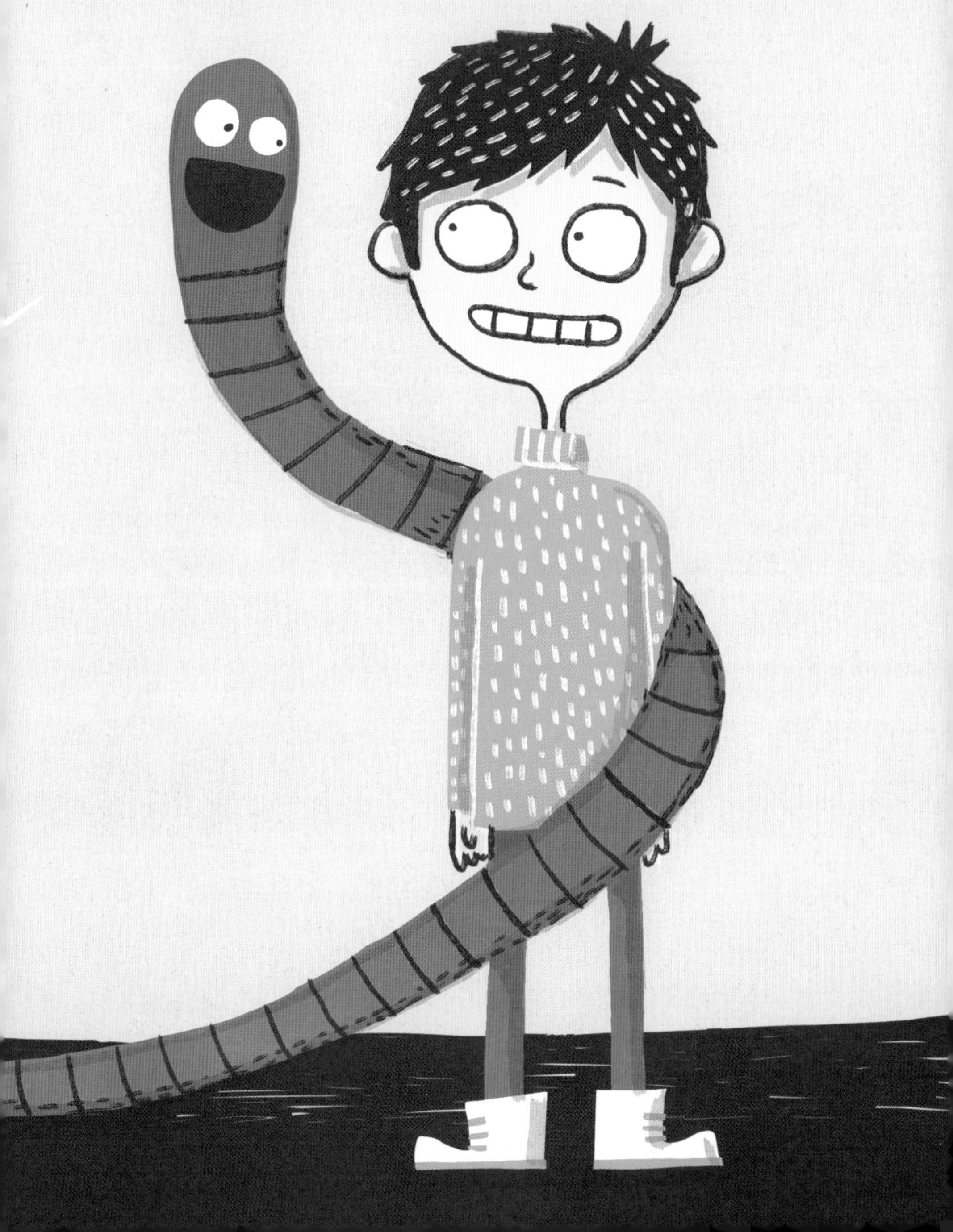

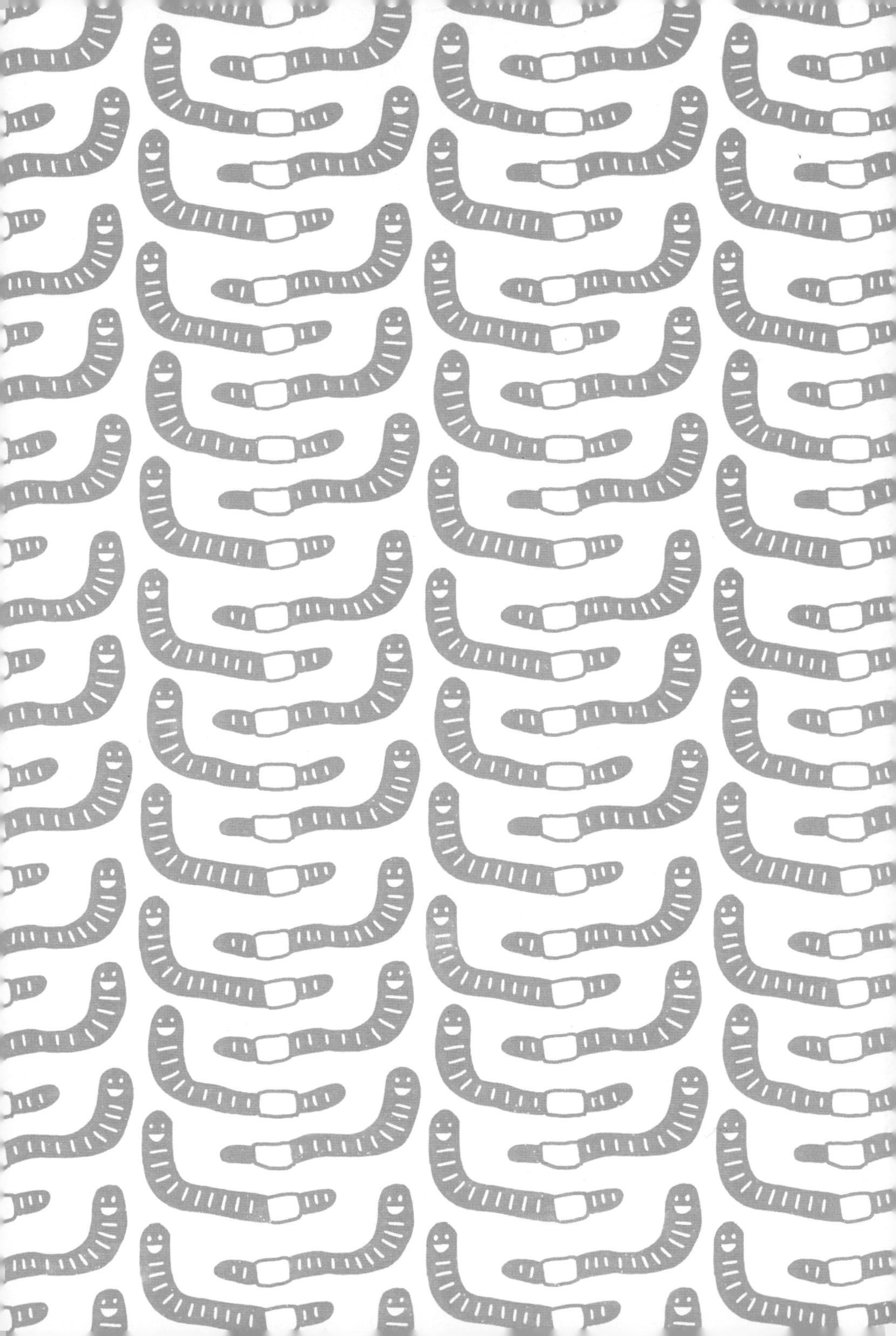

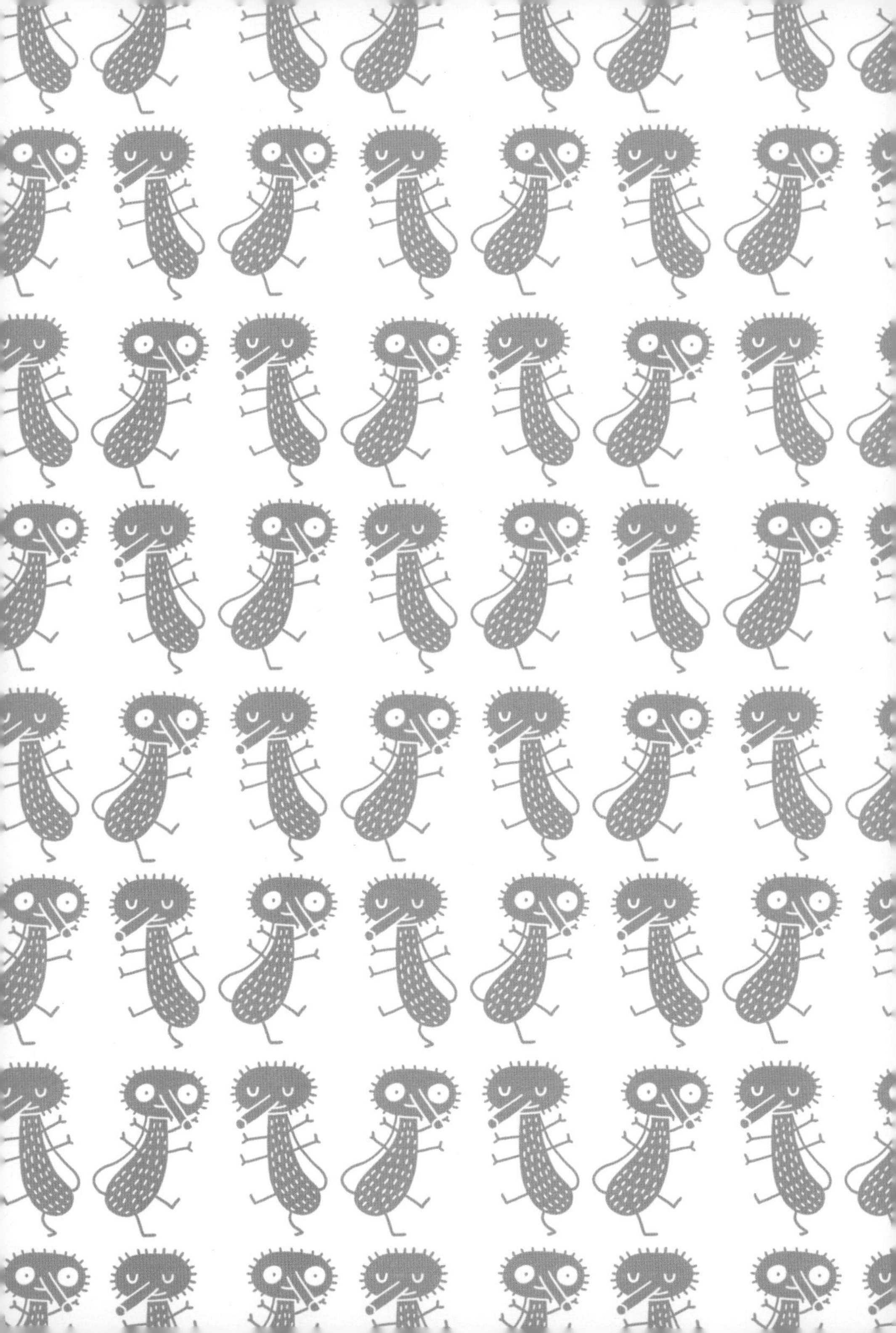

THE FLY

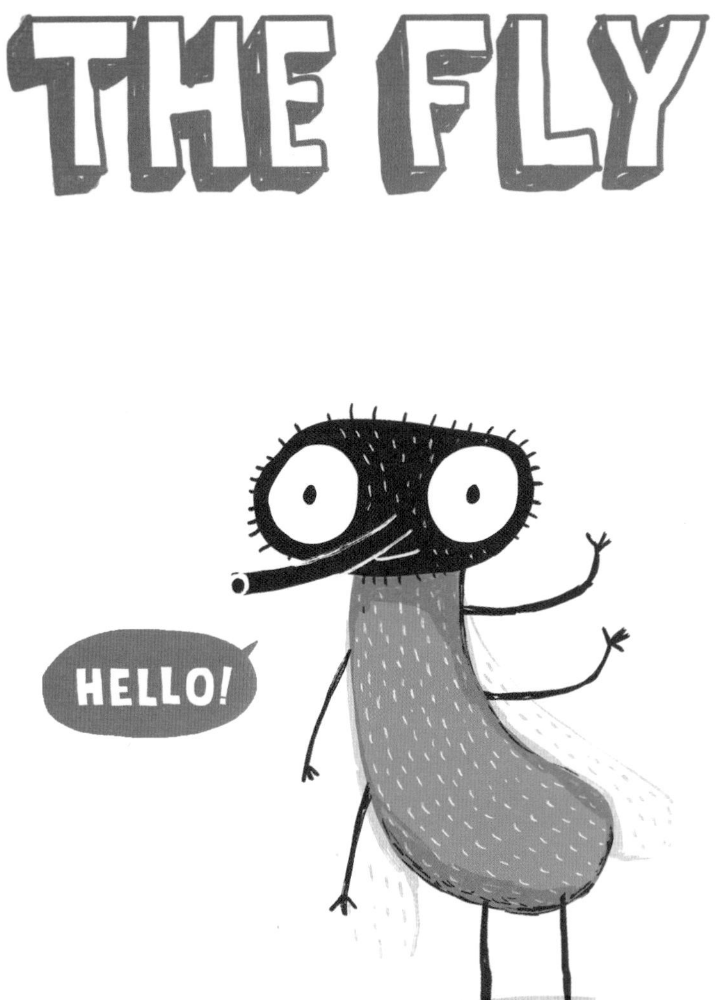
HELLO!

Let me introduce you
to a very special guy.

HERE'S

THE FLY.

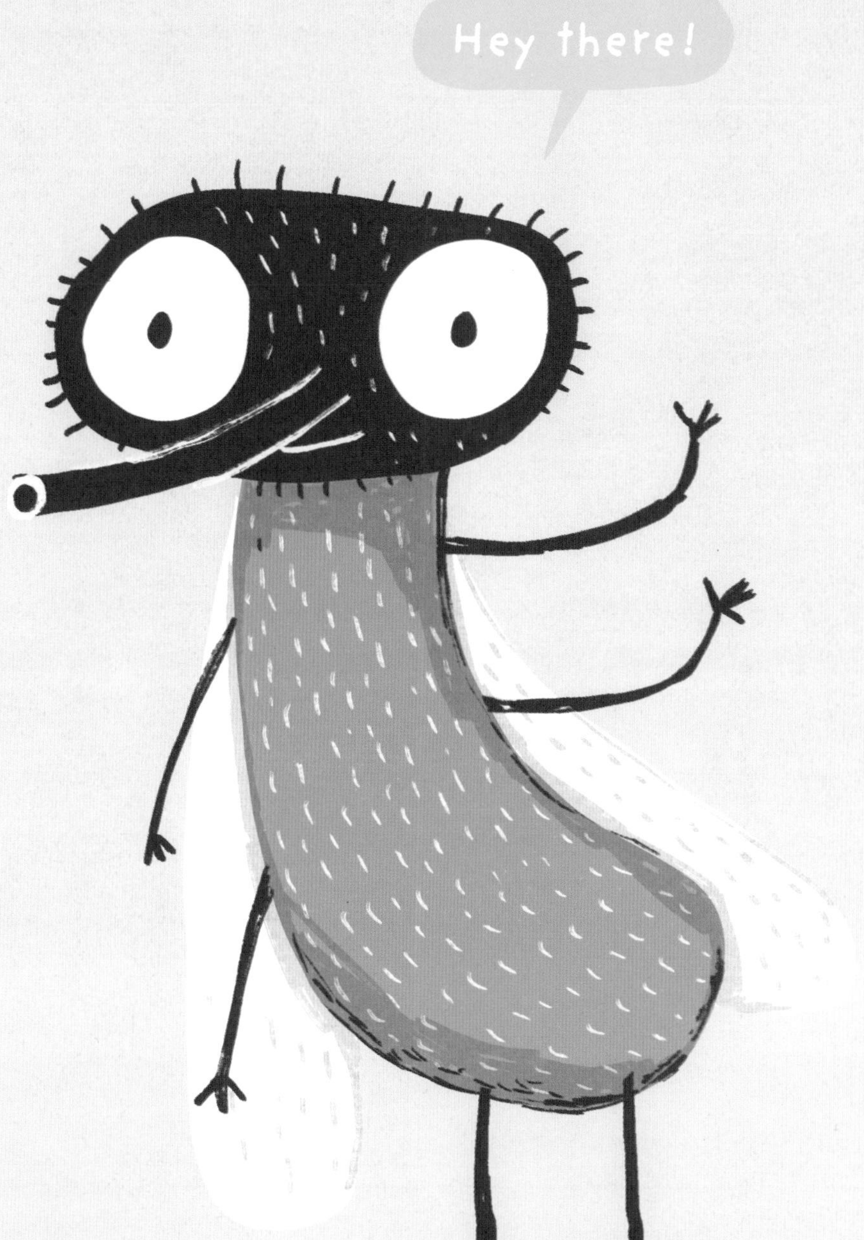
Hey there!

There are more than

100,000 SPECIES OF FLIES

in the world.

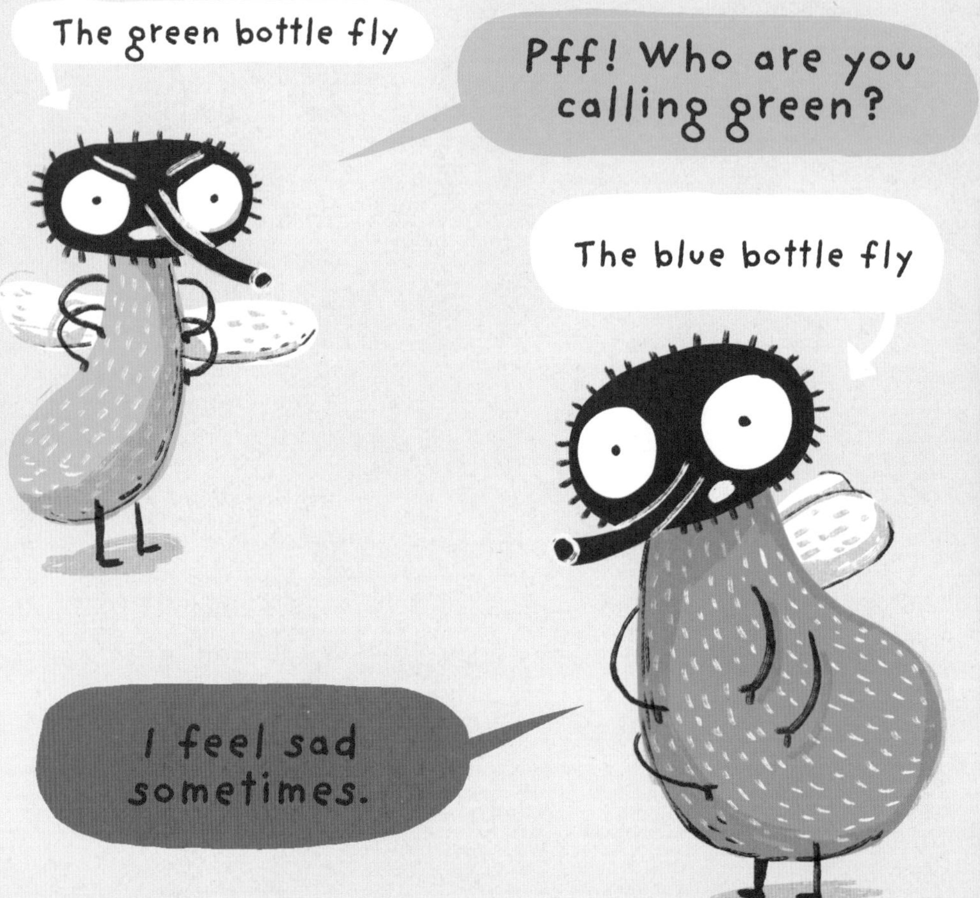
The green bottle fly
Pff! Who are you calling green?
The blue bottle fly
I feel sad sometimes.

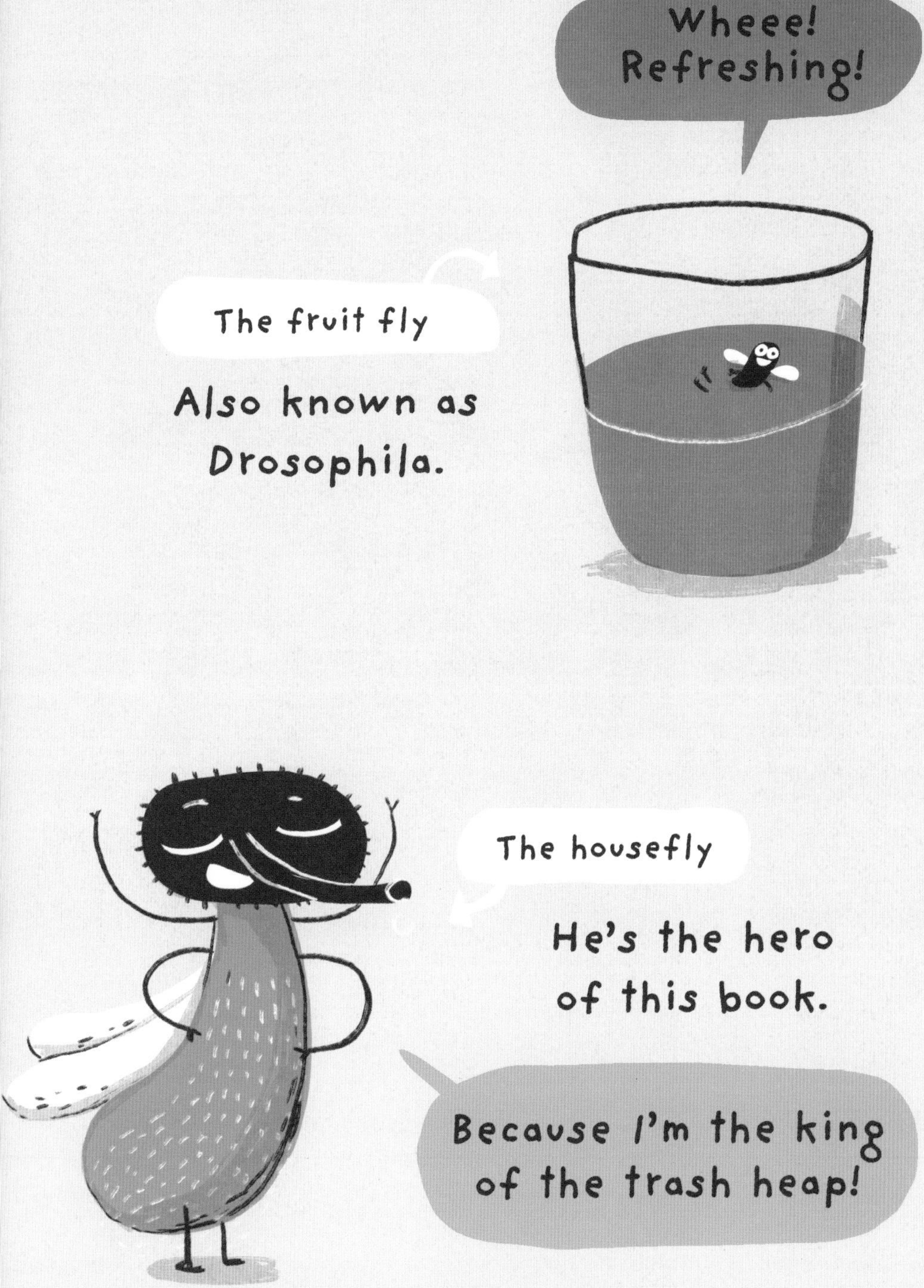
Wheee! Refreshing!
The fruit fly
Also known as Drosophila.
The housefly
He's the hero of this book.
Because I'm the king of the trash heap!

The housefly is a member of the

MUSCIDAE FAMILY.

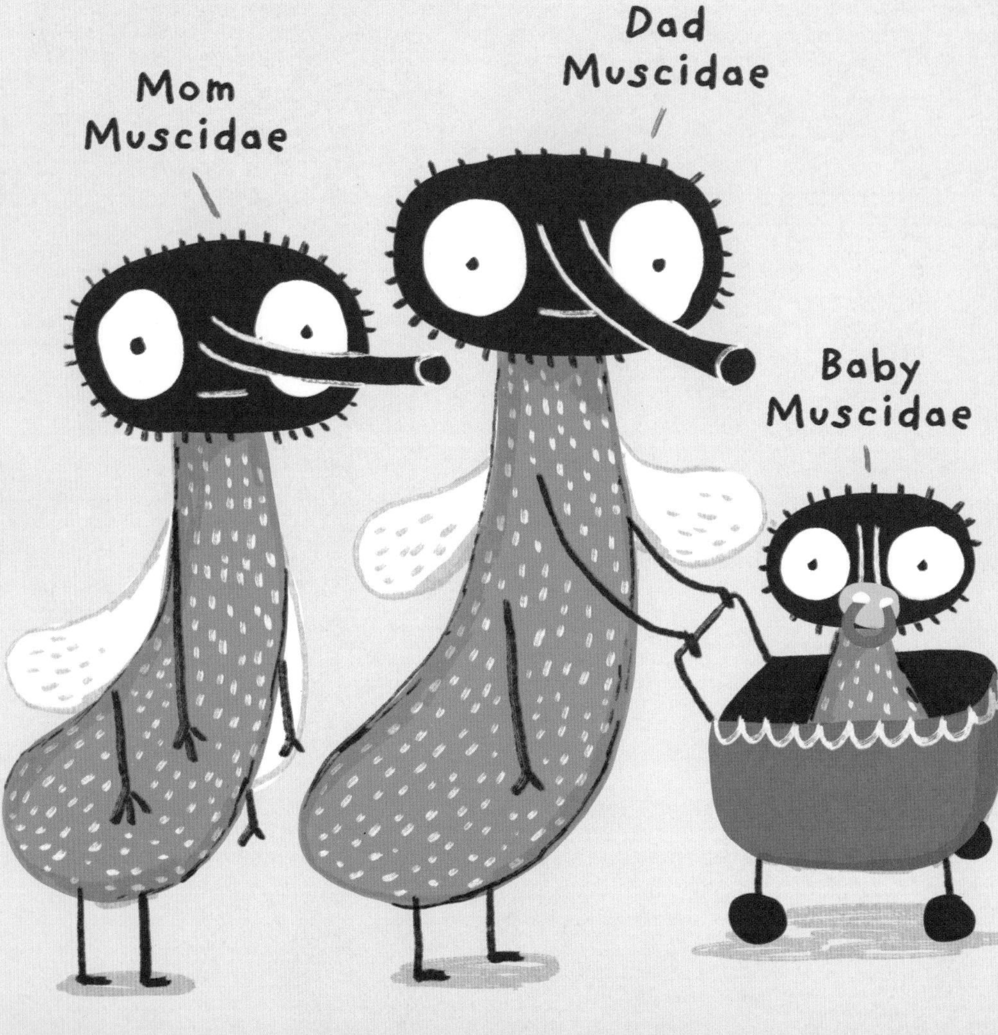
Mom Muscidae
Dad Muscidae
Baby Muscidae

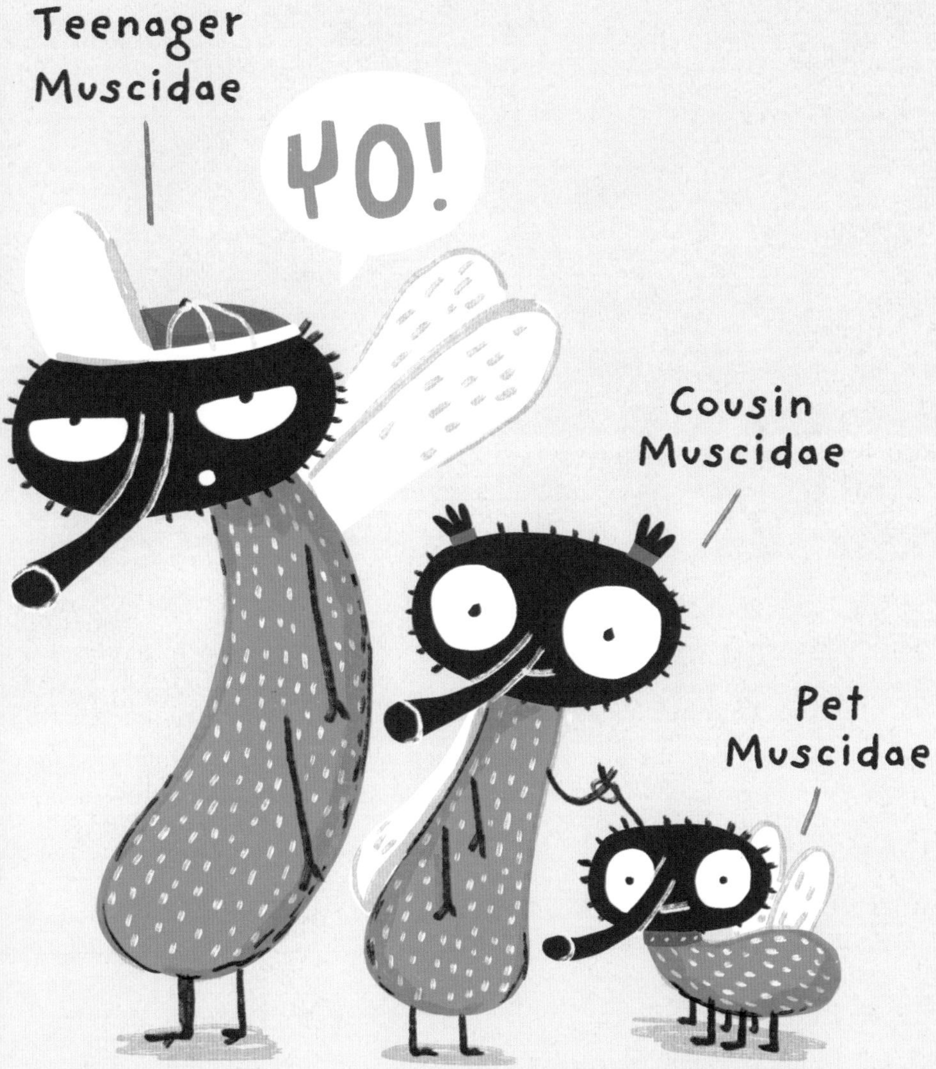
Teenager Muscidae
YO!
Cousin Muscidae
Pet Muscidae

We don't call him the

HOUSEFLY

because he's a pet, like a dog or cat,
but because he likes to get inside our

HOUSES.

Hey, I'm not a DOG!

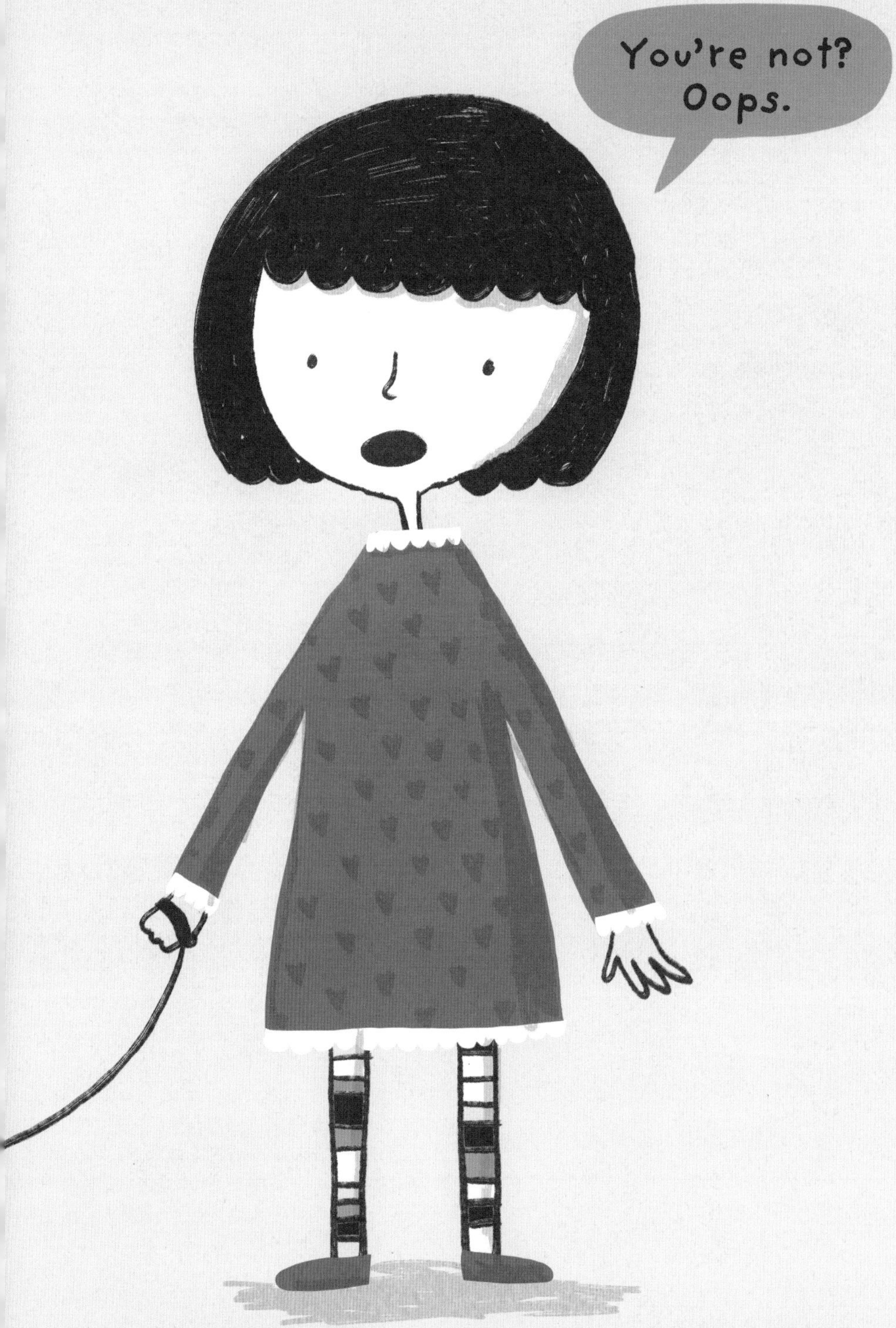
You're not? Oops.

The housefly is found in every country in the world. Houseflies like humans because we offer them a warm place to live and lots of

GARBAGE TO EAT.

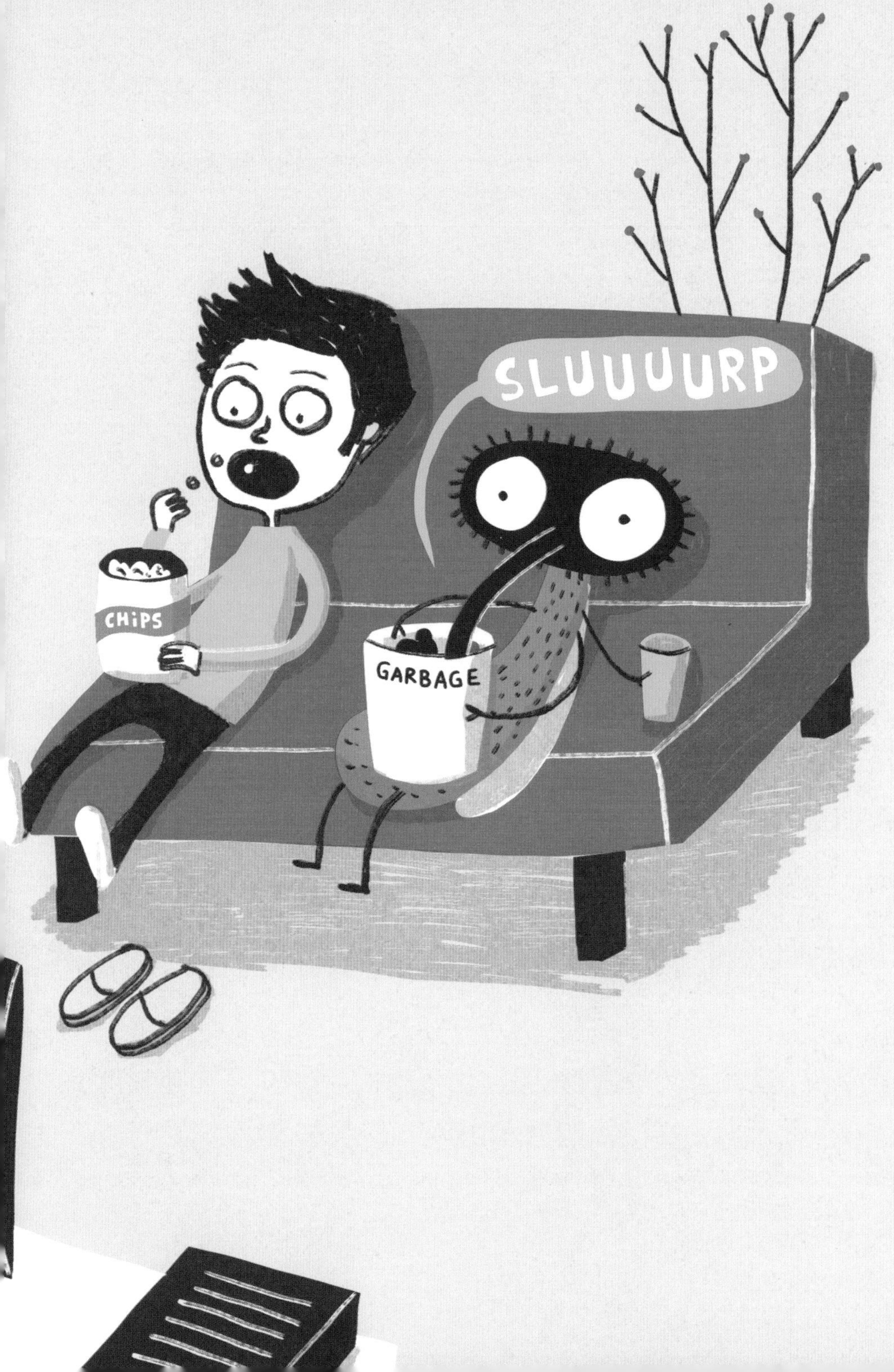
SLUUUURP
CHIPS
GARBAGE

The housefly is gray, with black stripes on his back, and his body is

COVERED WITH HAIR.

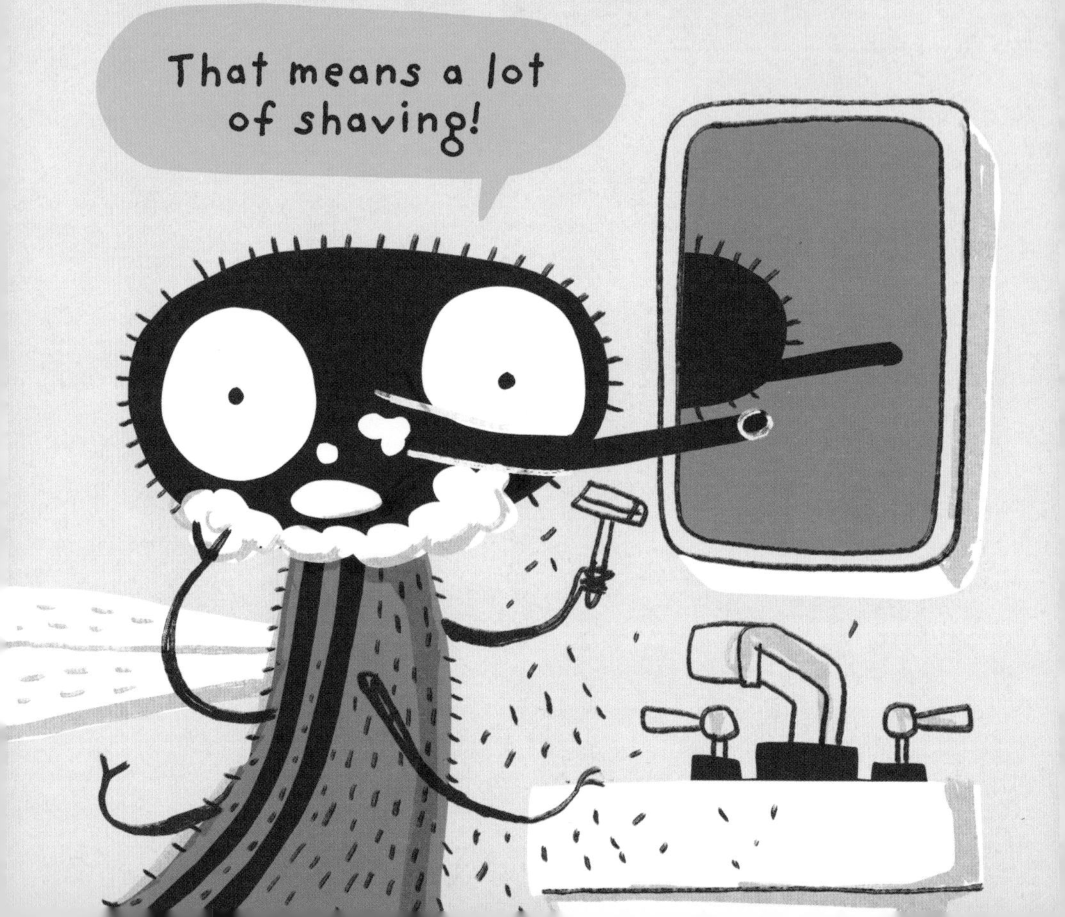
That means a lot of shaving!

The housefly measures from 0.2 to 0.3 inches (5 to 8 millimeters) long. The female is slightly bigger than the male.

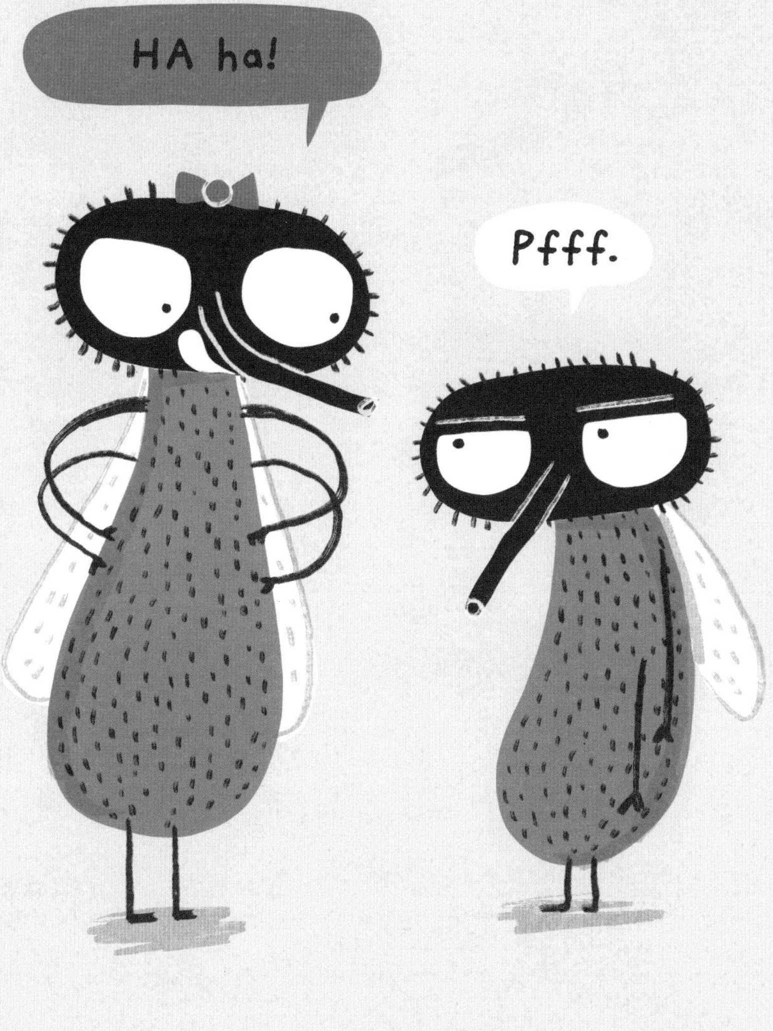
HA ha!
Pfff.

The housefly's eyes are red and have many tiny flat surfaces that allow him to see in all directions at the same time.

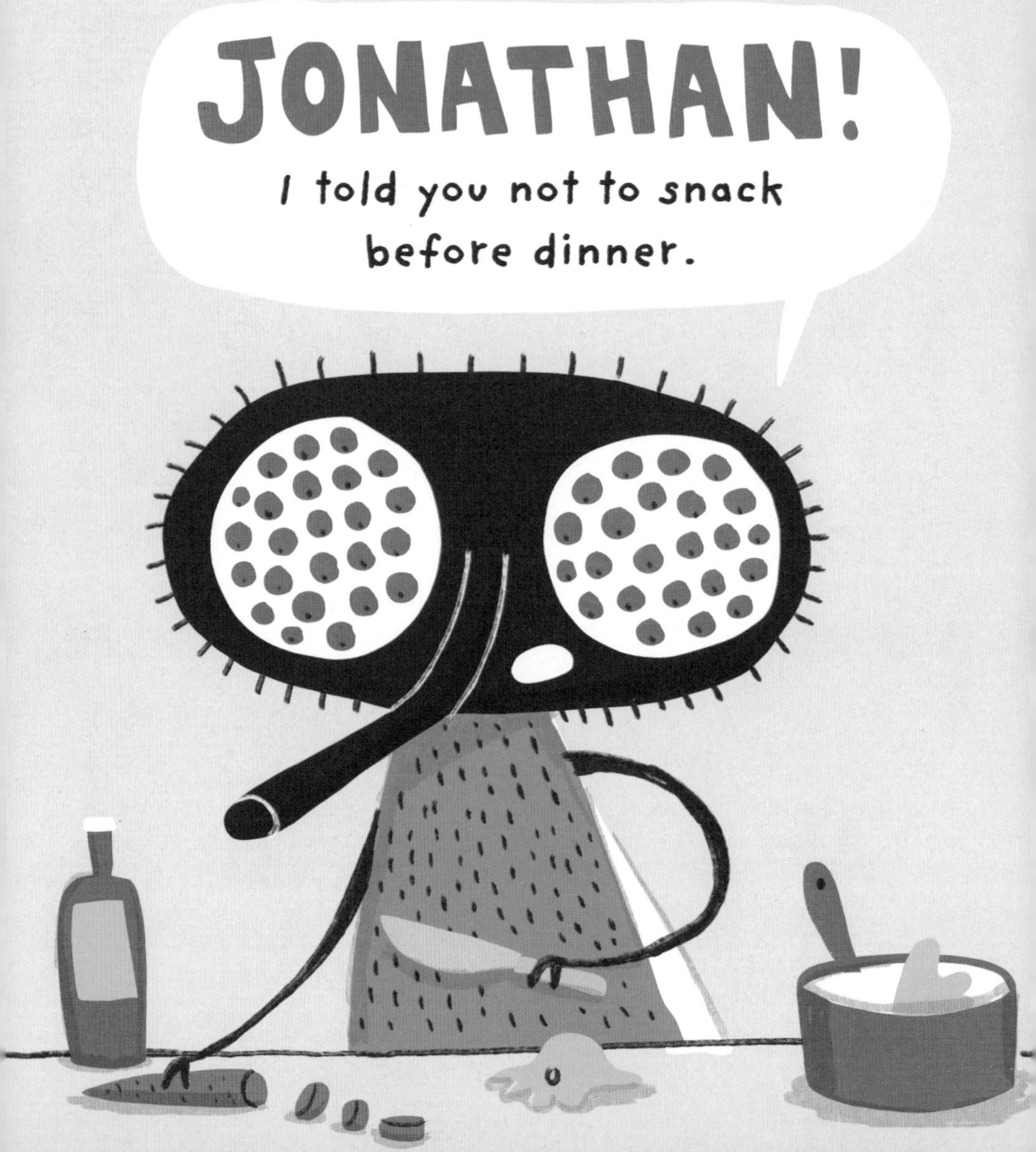
JONATHAN!
I told you not to snack before dinner.

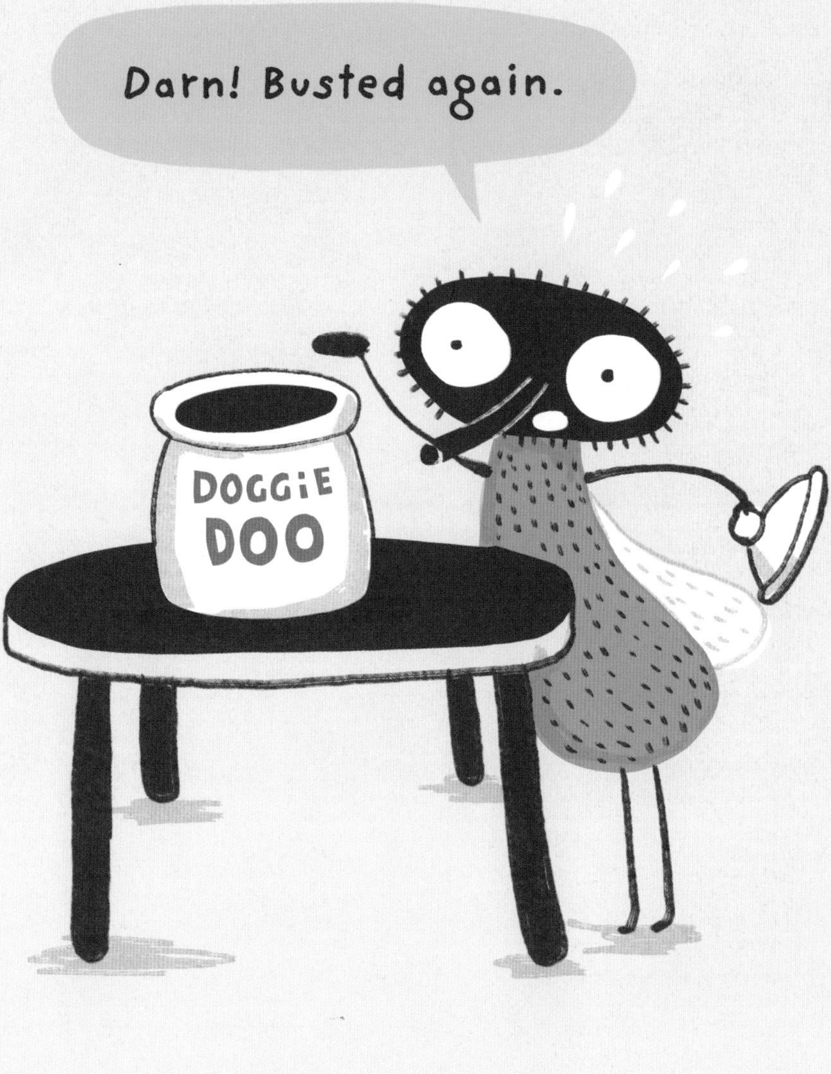
Darn! Busted again.
DOGGIE DOO

Thanks to little

BUBBLES OF LIQUID

at the ends of his feet, the housefly
can walk on walls or even on the

CEILING.

It's pretty cool,
but it's not easy to
play soccer up here.

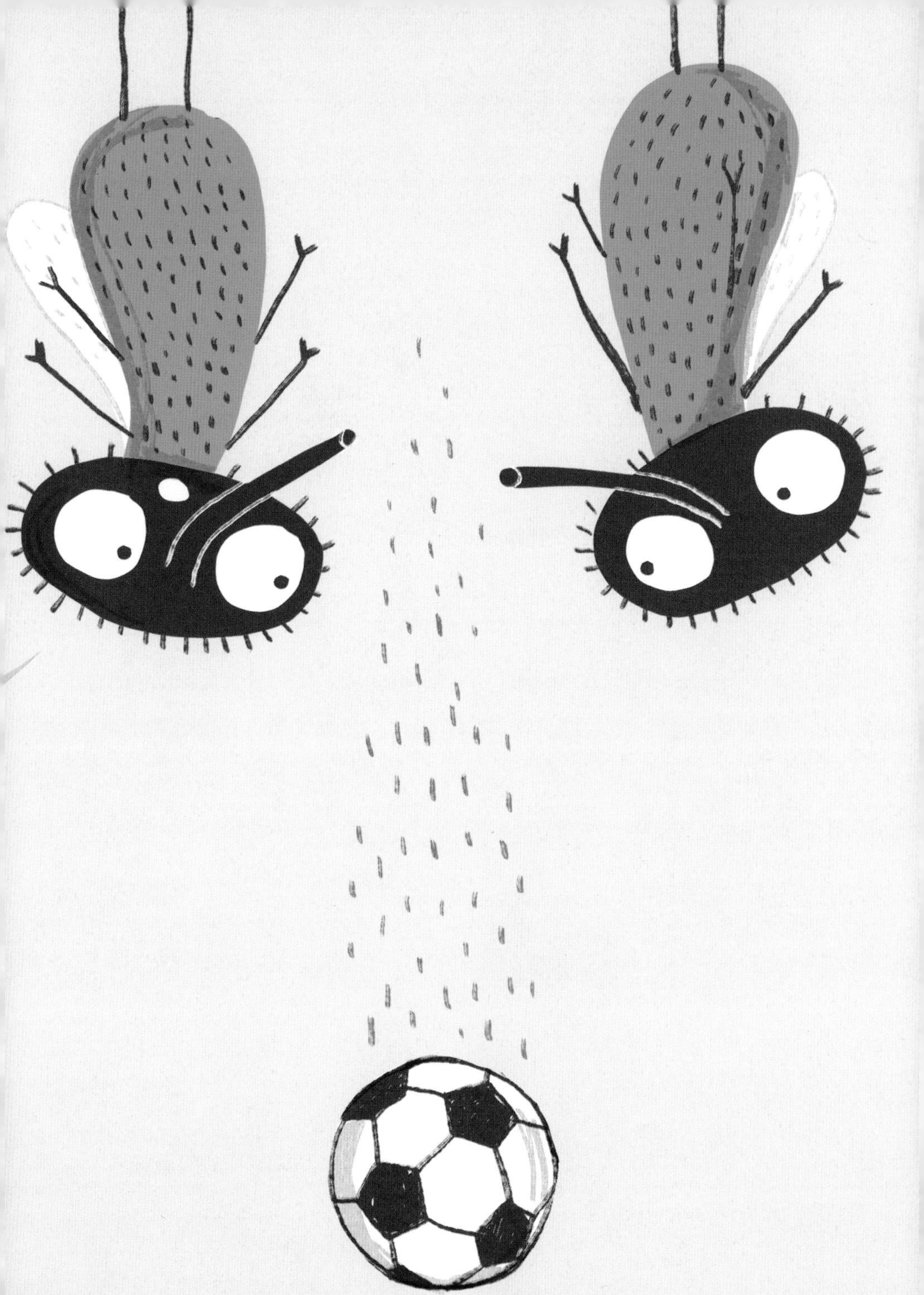

The housefly uses his tube-shaped mouth to suck up his food. He can only eat

LIQUID FOODS, or just LIQUID,

so he spits or vomits a bit of digestive fluid on his meal to soften it.

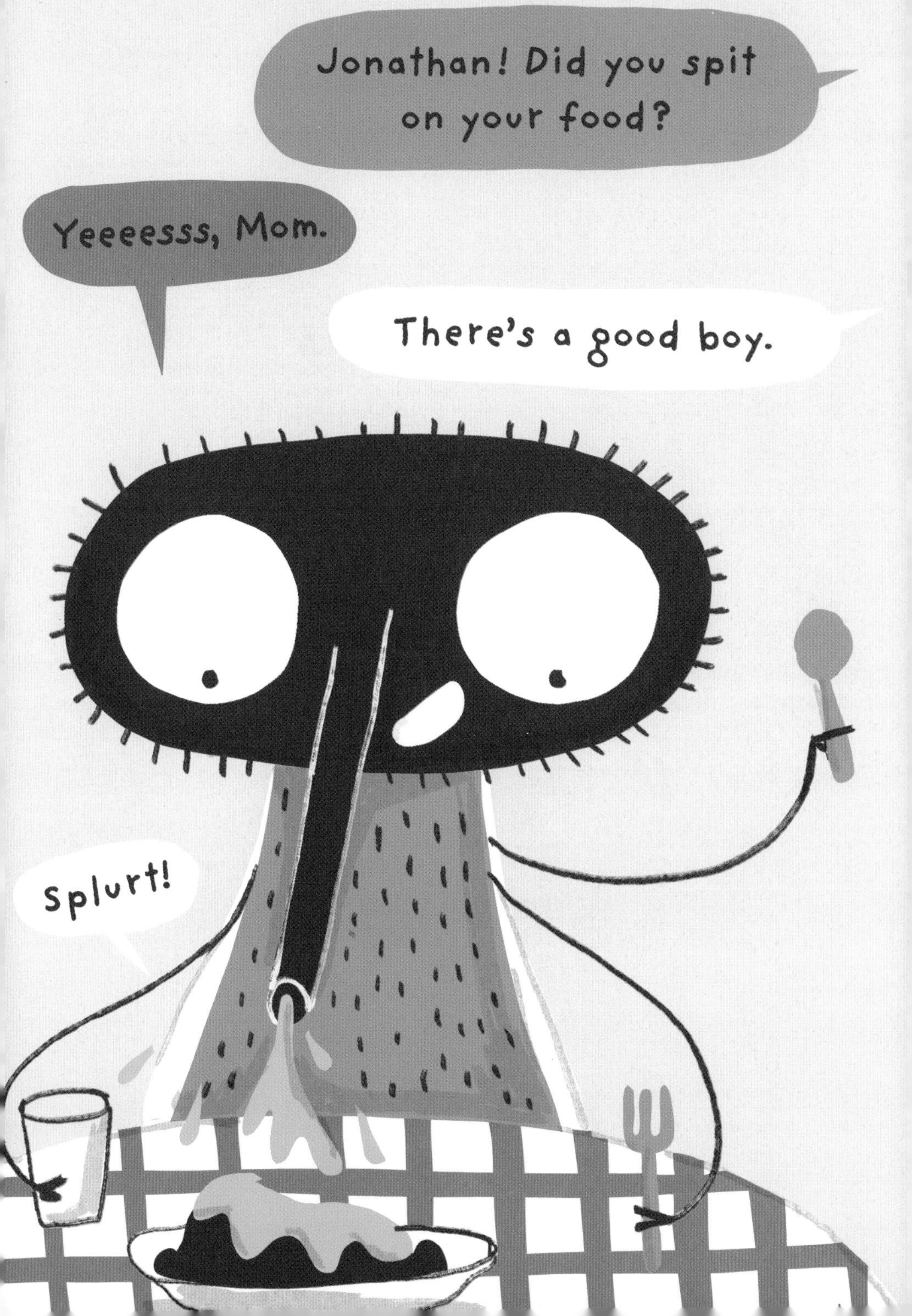
Jonathan! Did you spit on your food?
Yeeeesss, Mom.
There's a good boy.
Splurt!

The fly has really

DISGUSTING TASTE IN FOOD.

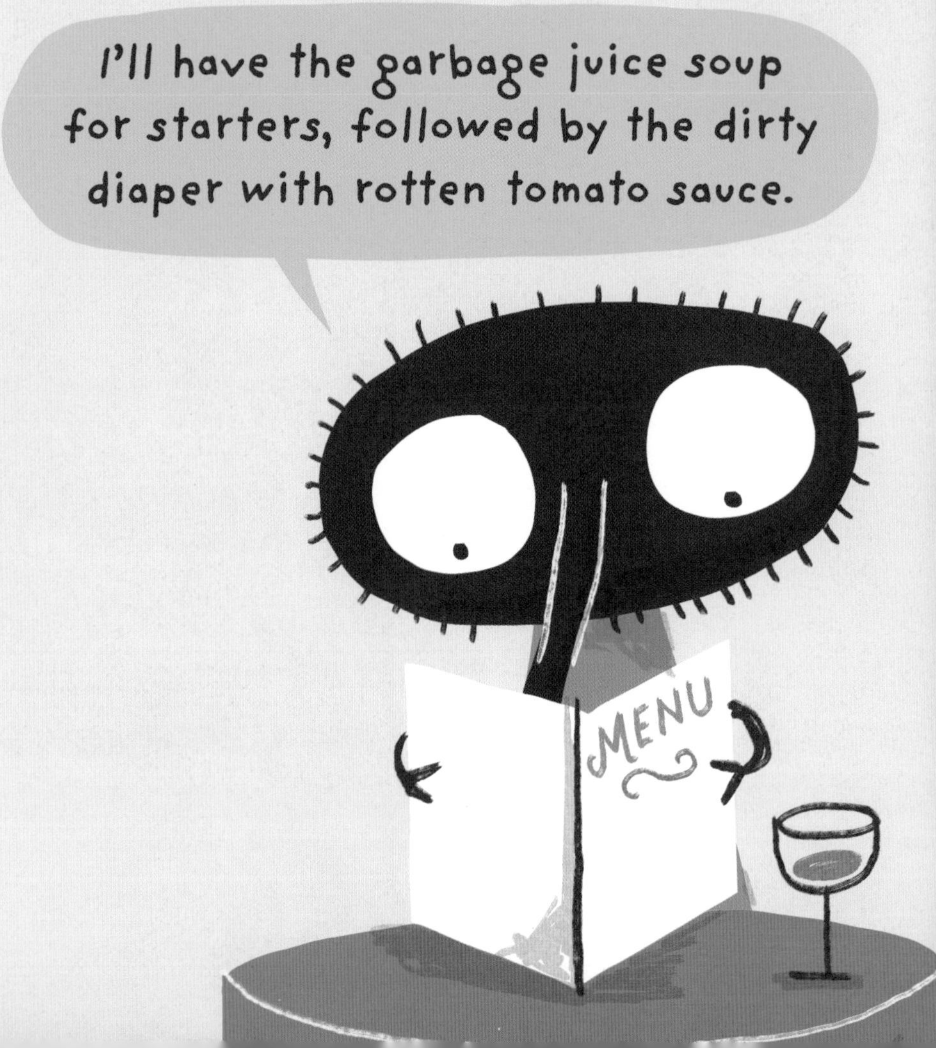
I'll have the garbage juice soup for starters, followed by the dirty diaper with rotten tomato sauce.
MENU

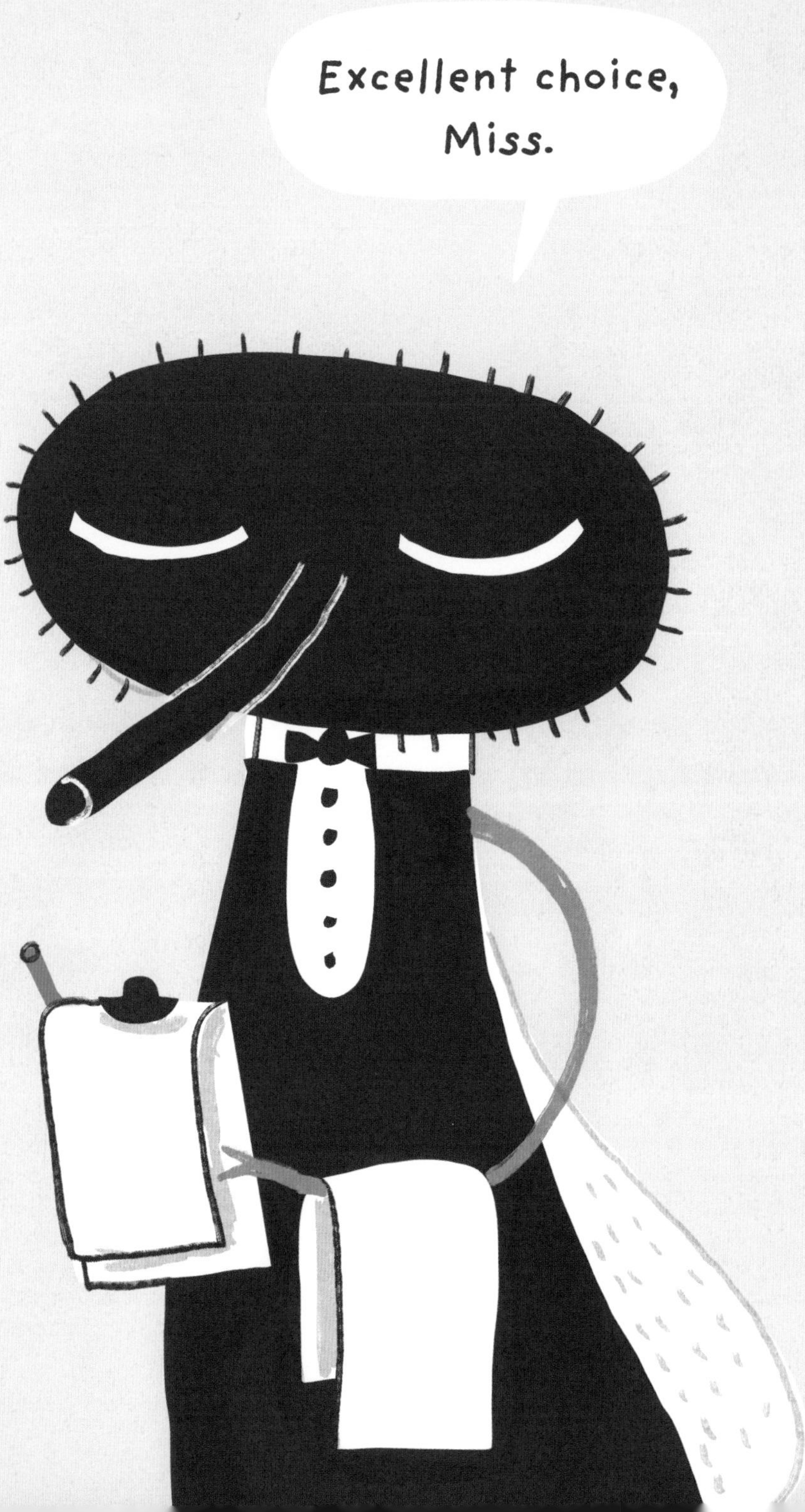
Excellent choice, Miss.

The female fly can lay over a hundred eggs at a time. From the egg comes a maggot, which then turns into a pupa, which then becomes a fly.

1

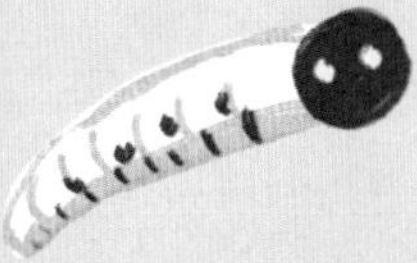

MAGGOT

2

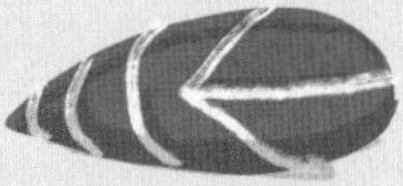

PUPA

3

FLY

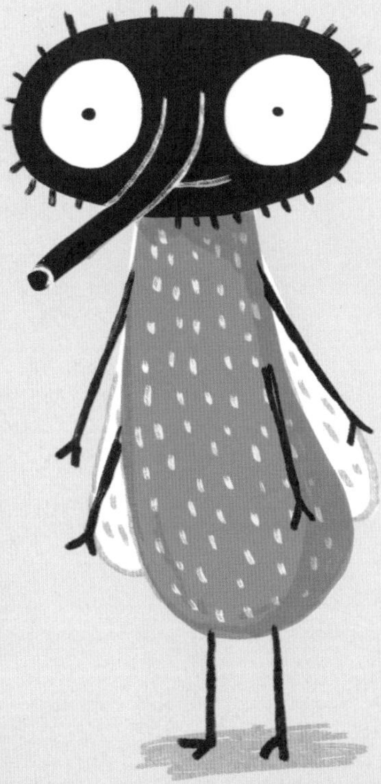

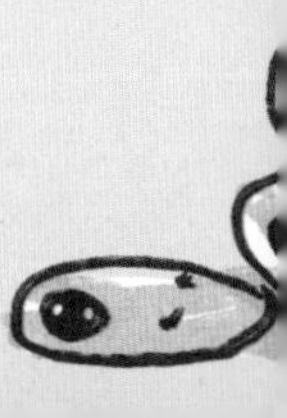

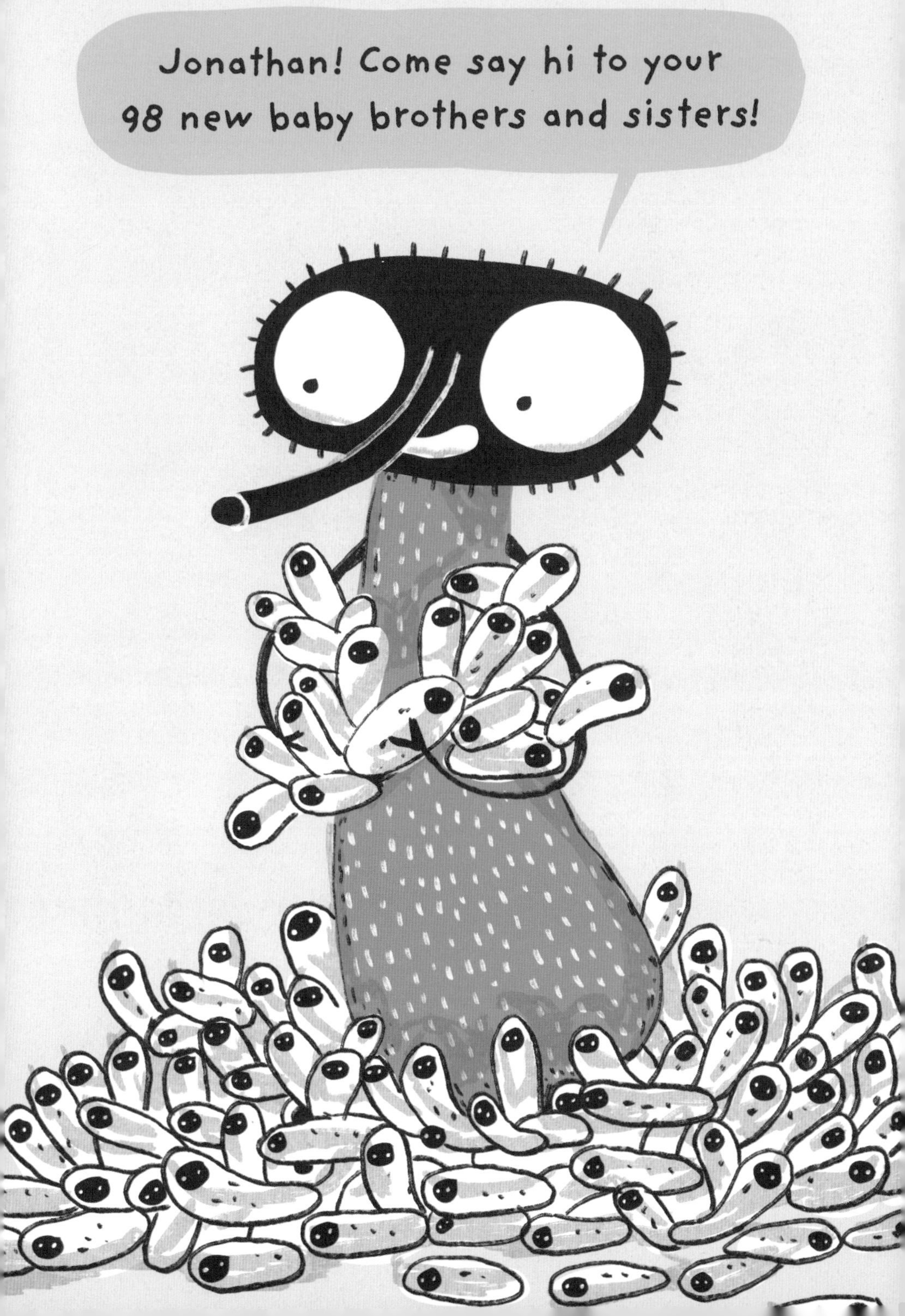
Jonathan! Come say hi to your 98 new baby brothers and sisters!

The fly can be eaten by other insects, such as spiders, or by birds or fish. The fly lives between

15 AND 30 DAYS.

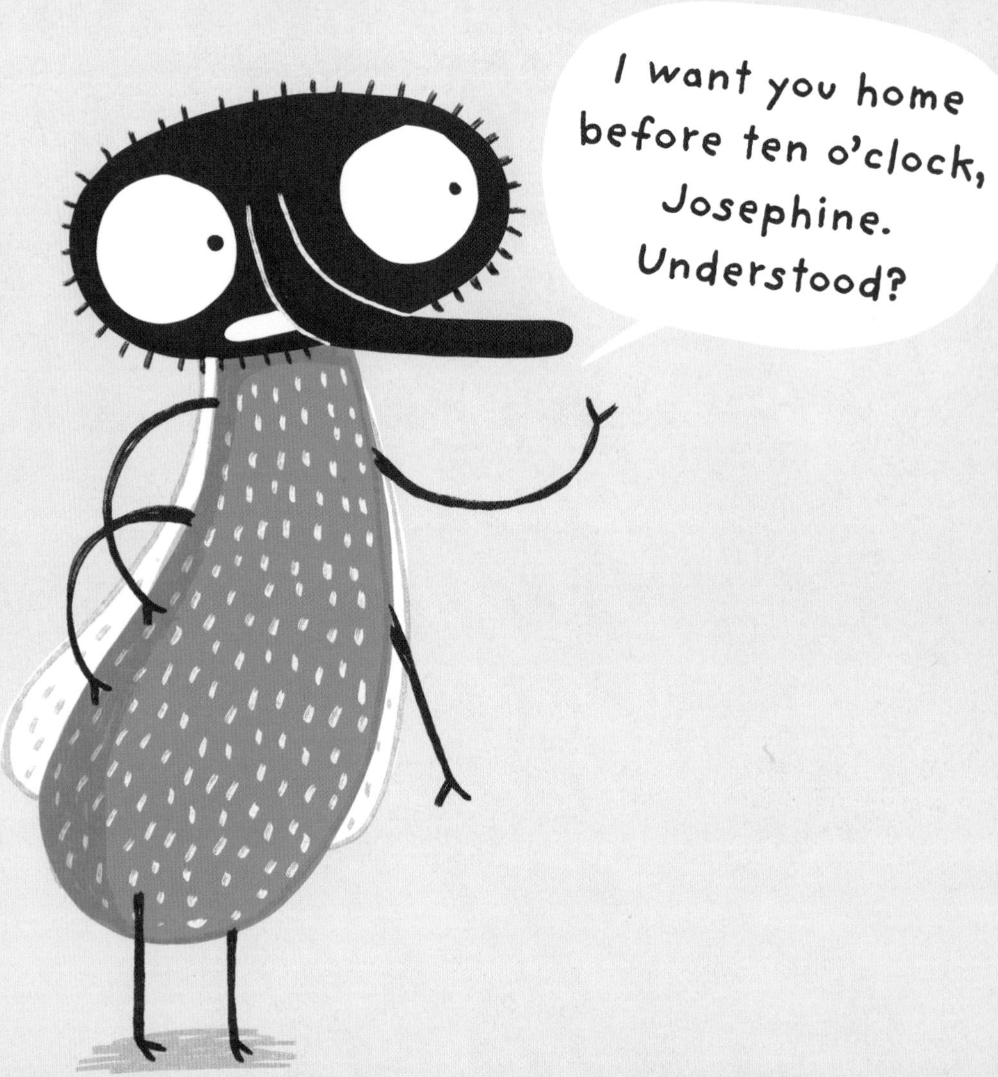
I want you home before ten o'clock, Josephine. Understood?

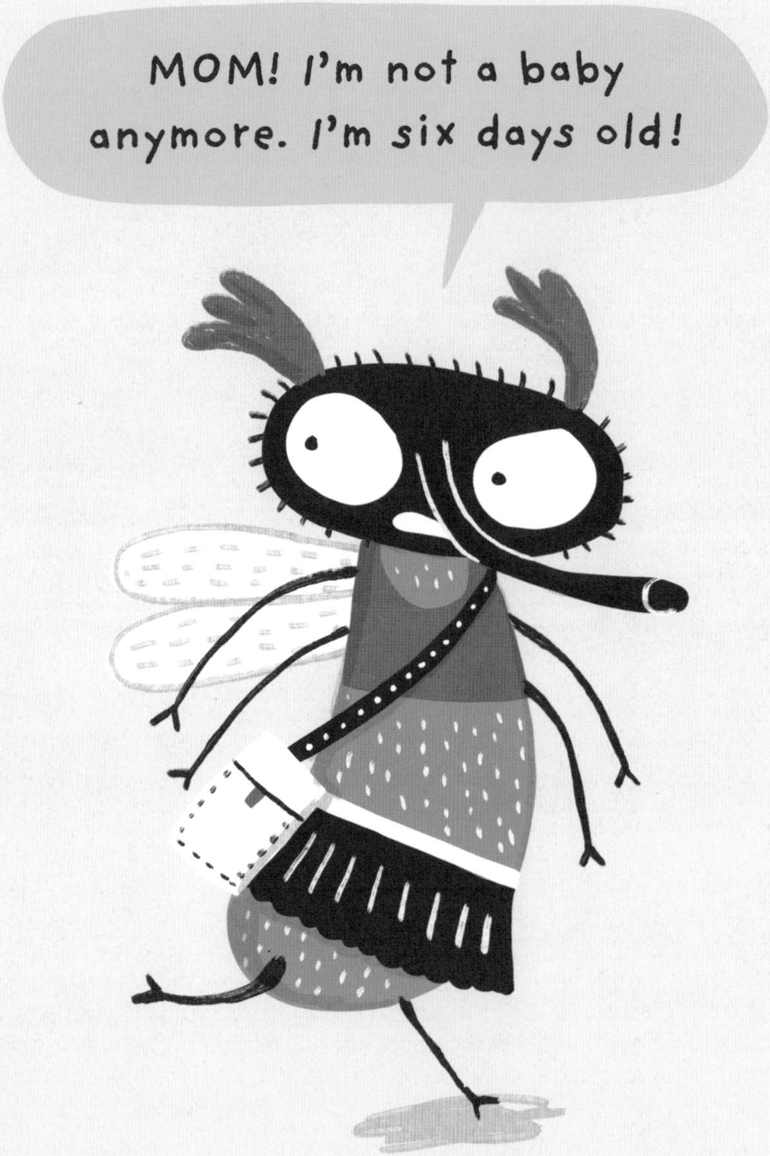
MOM! I'm not a baby anymore. I'm six days old!

Because he walks on garbage and gross stuff like poo, the fly can carry

GERMS

and cause hundreds of

DISEASES.

Good morning.
You ordered a flu?

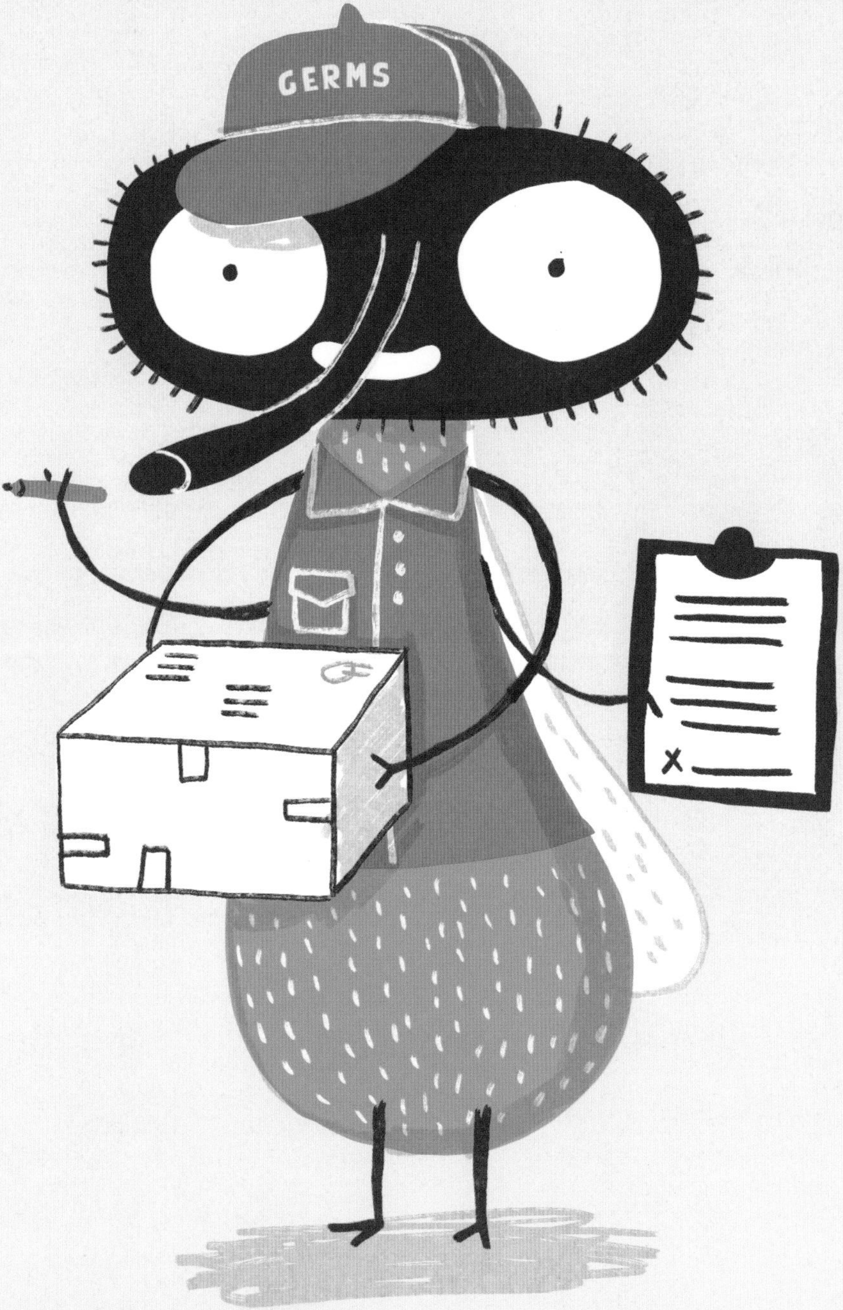
GERMS

So next time a fly wants to share your food, make sure he washes

HIS HANDS.

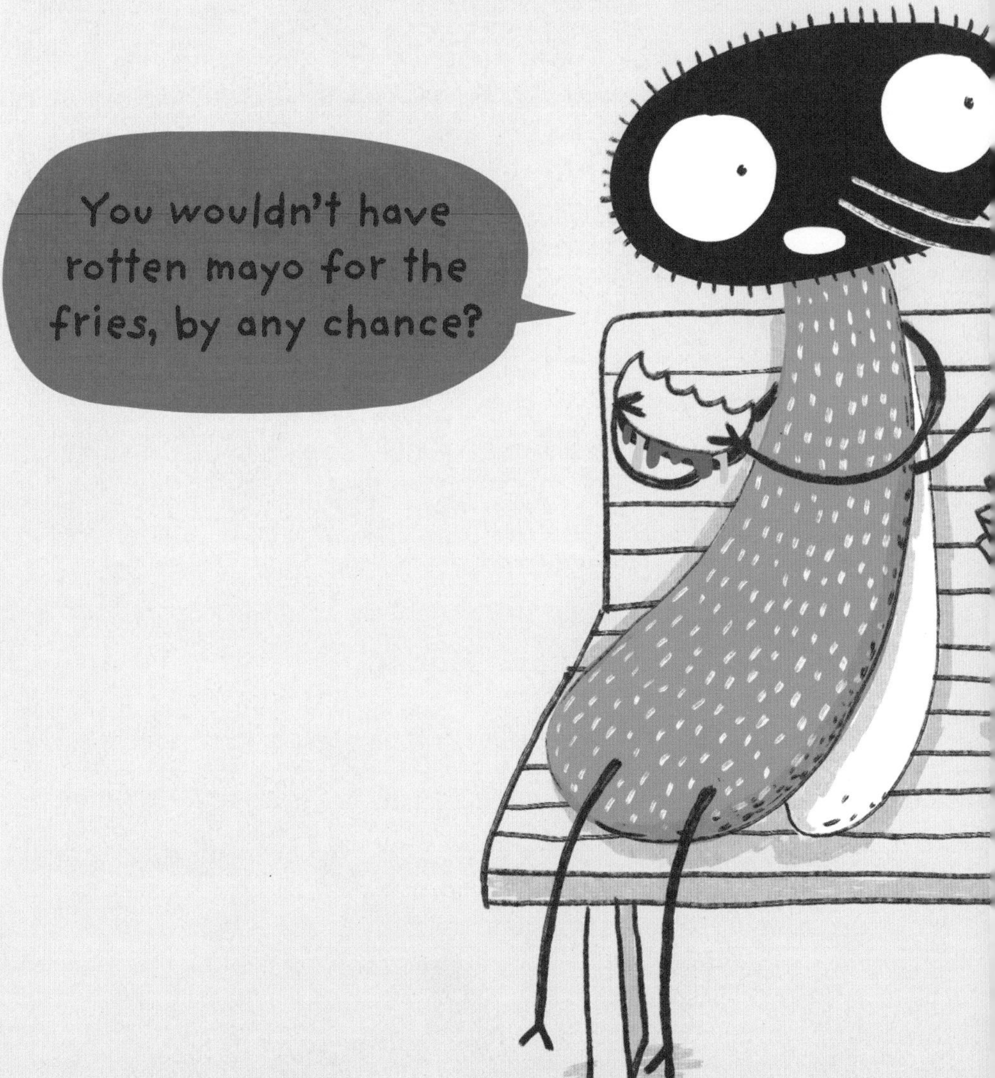
You wouldn't have rotten mayo for the fries, by any chance?

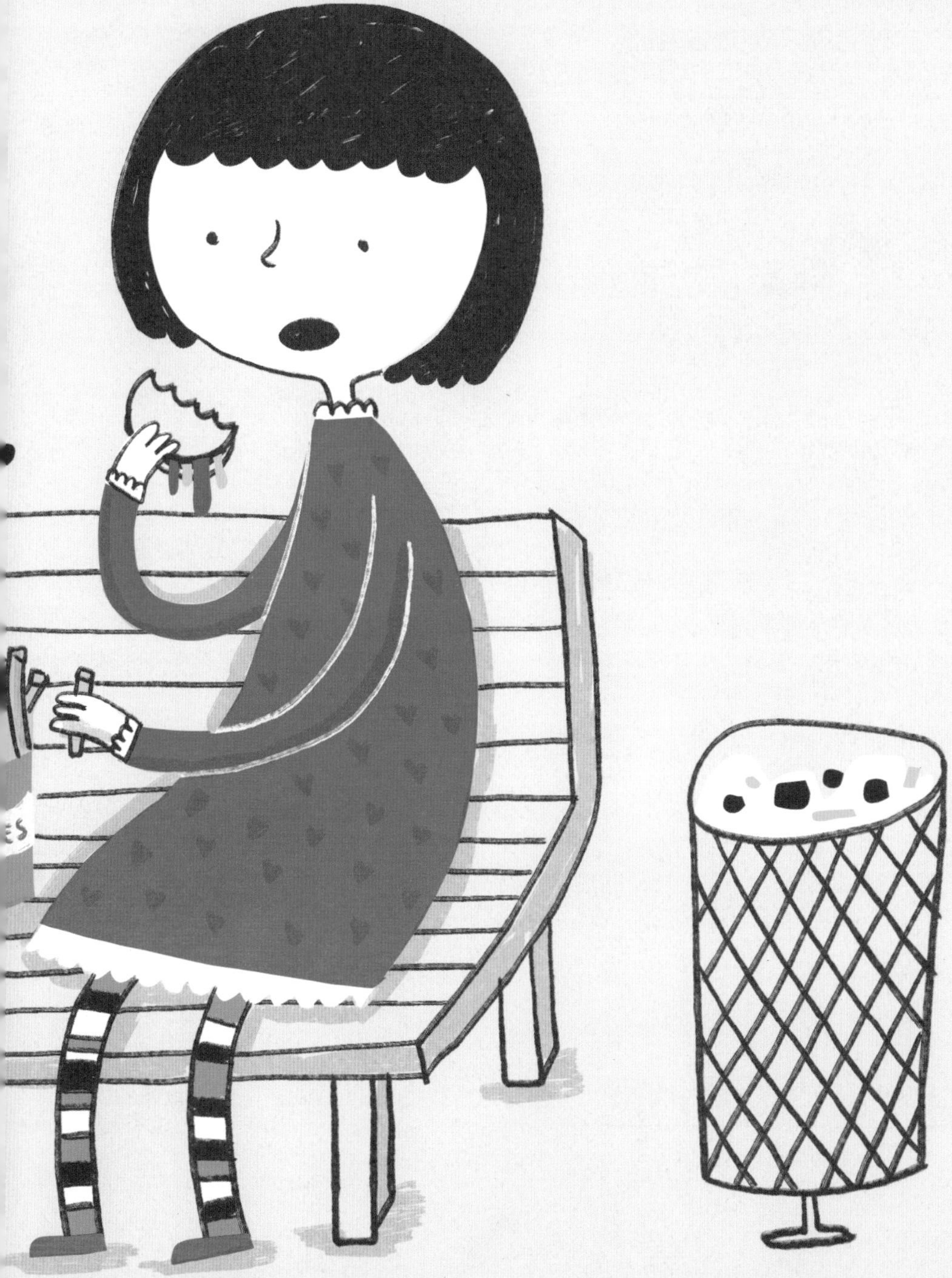

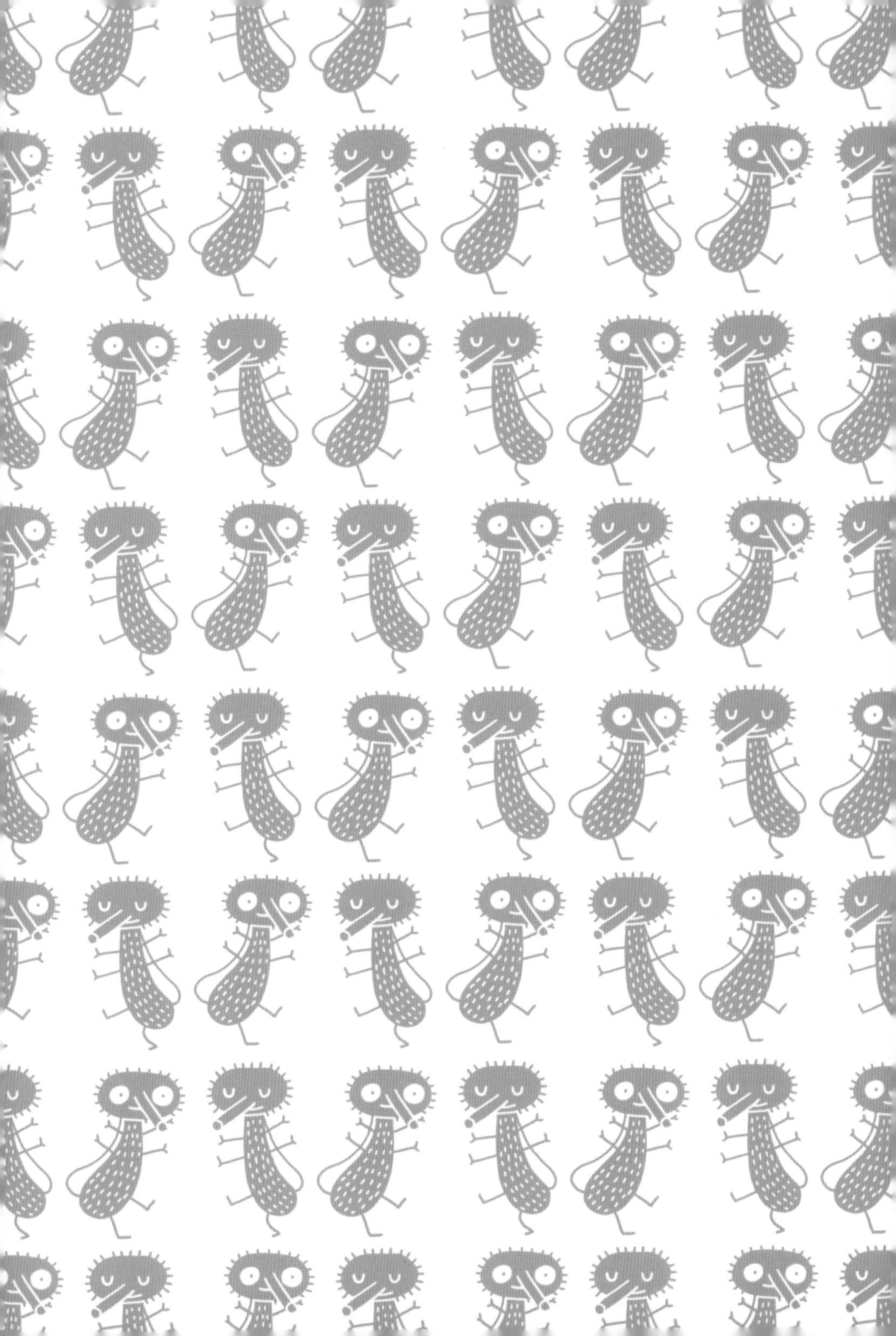

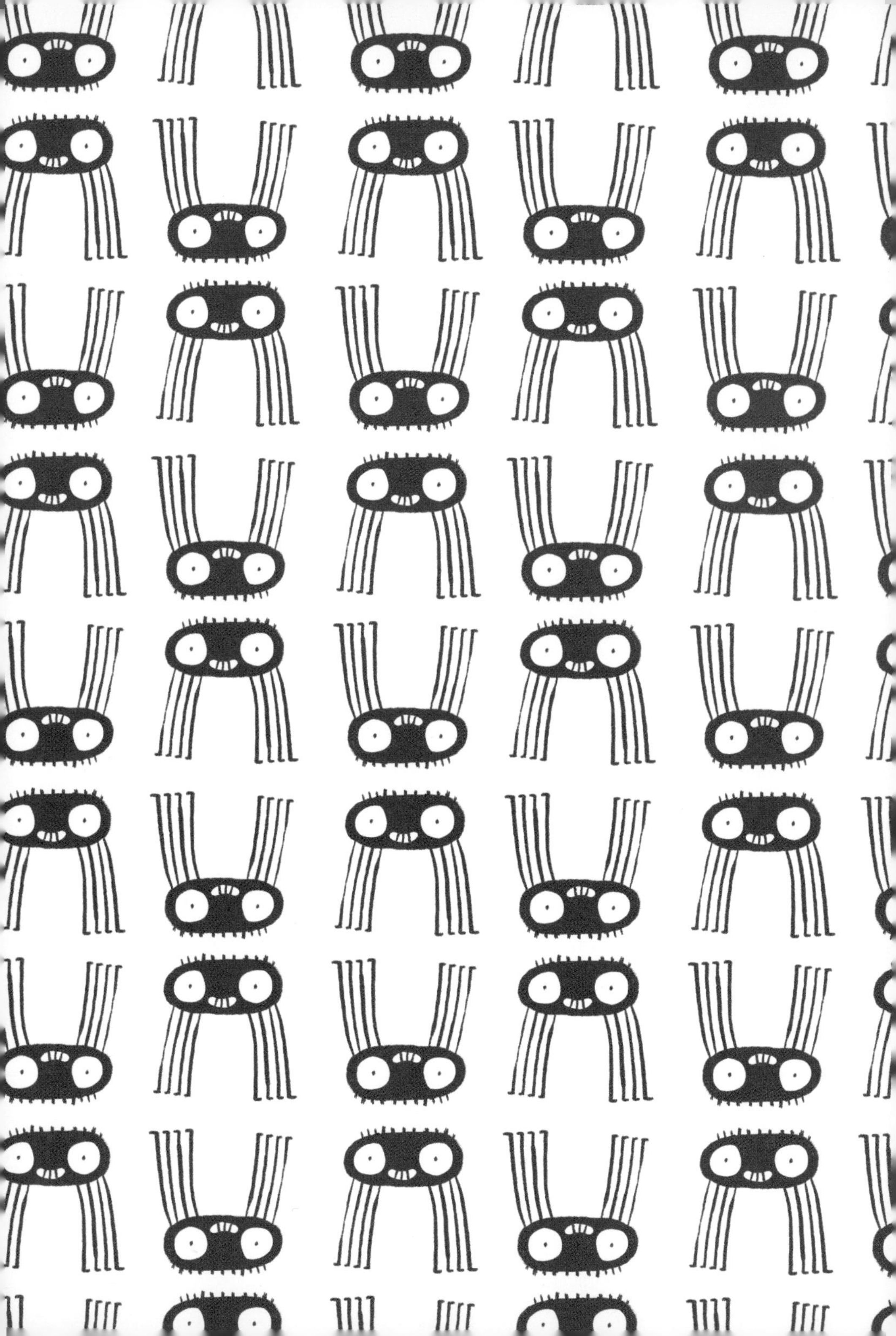

THE SPIDER

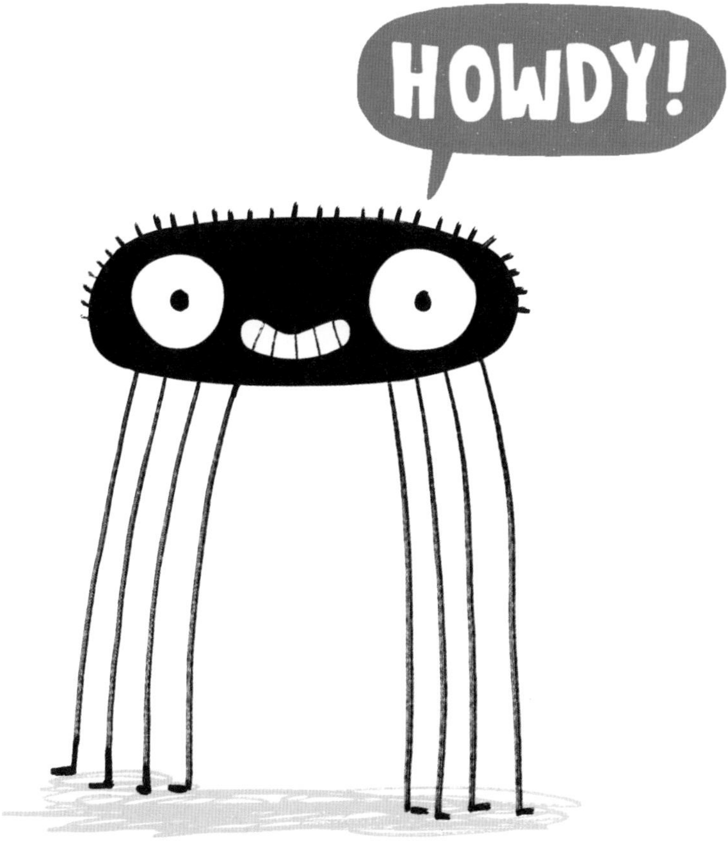
HOWDY!

Ladies and gentlemen, please welcome your friend

THE SPiDER.

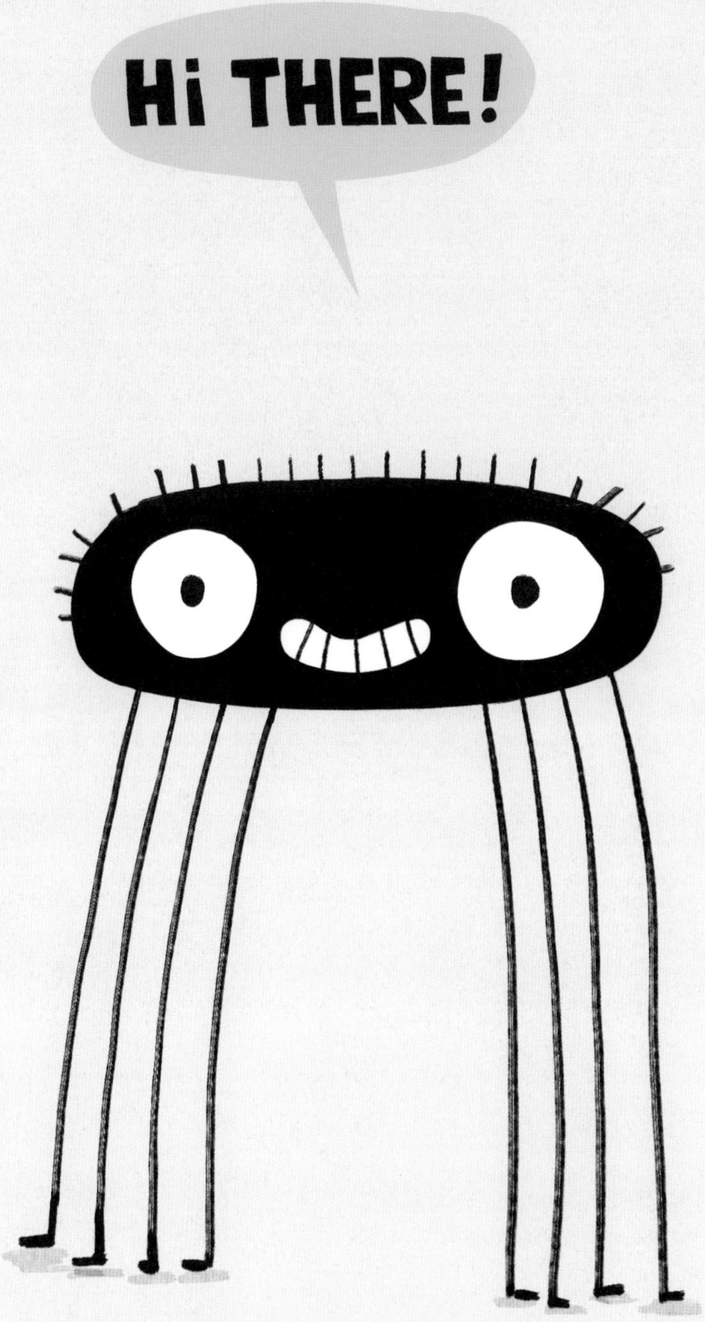
Hi THERE!

There are over 40,000 species of spiders. They can live in almost any environment:

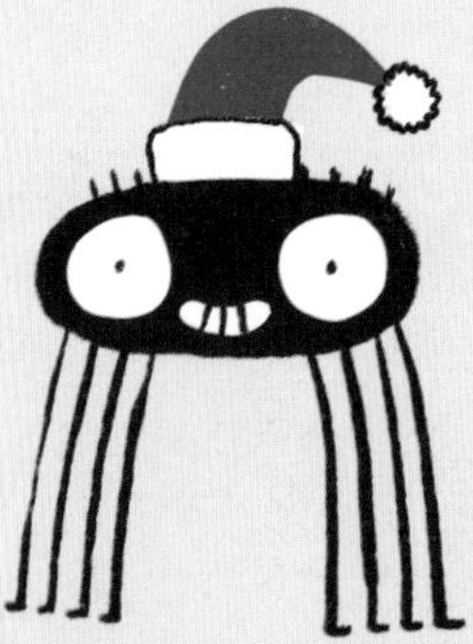

In cold climates

In warm climates

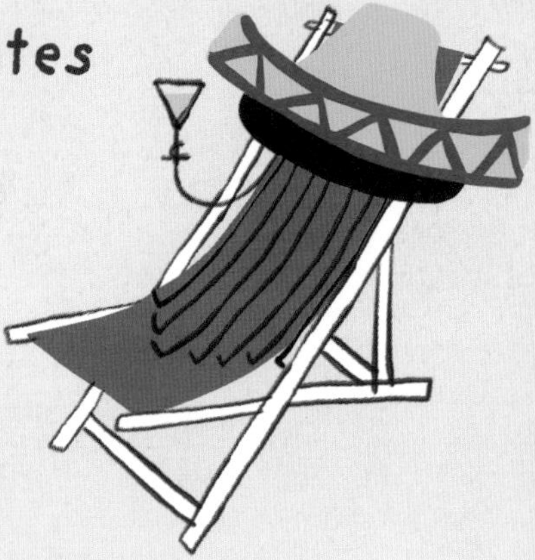

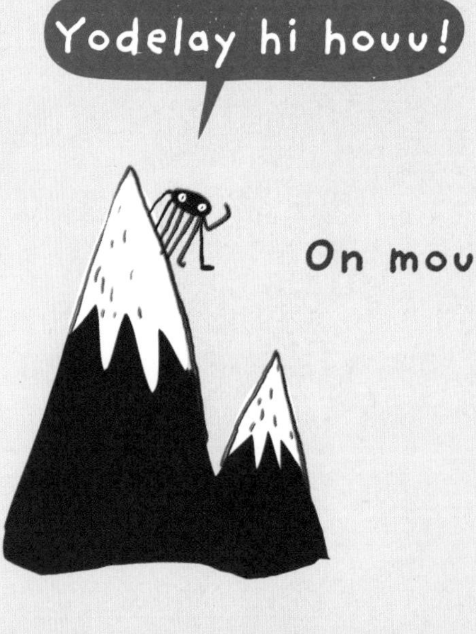
Yodelay hi houu!

On mountaintops

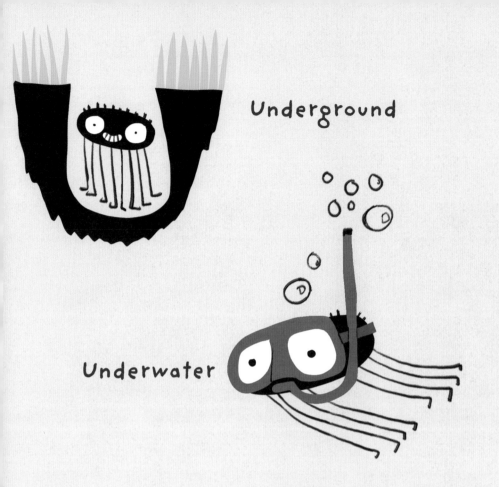

Underground

Underwater

. . . But not in outer space.

Darn it!

Since she has eight legs, the spider is not considered an

INSECT.

Insects only have six legs.

Maybe not, but I'm so pretty in princess shoes.

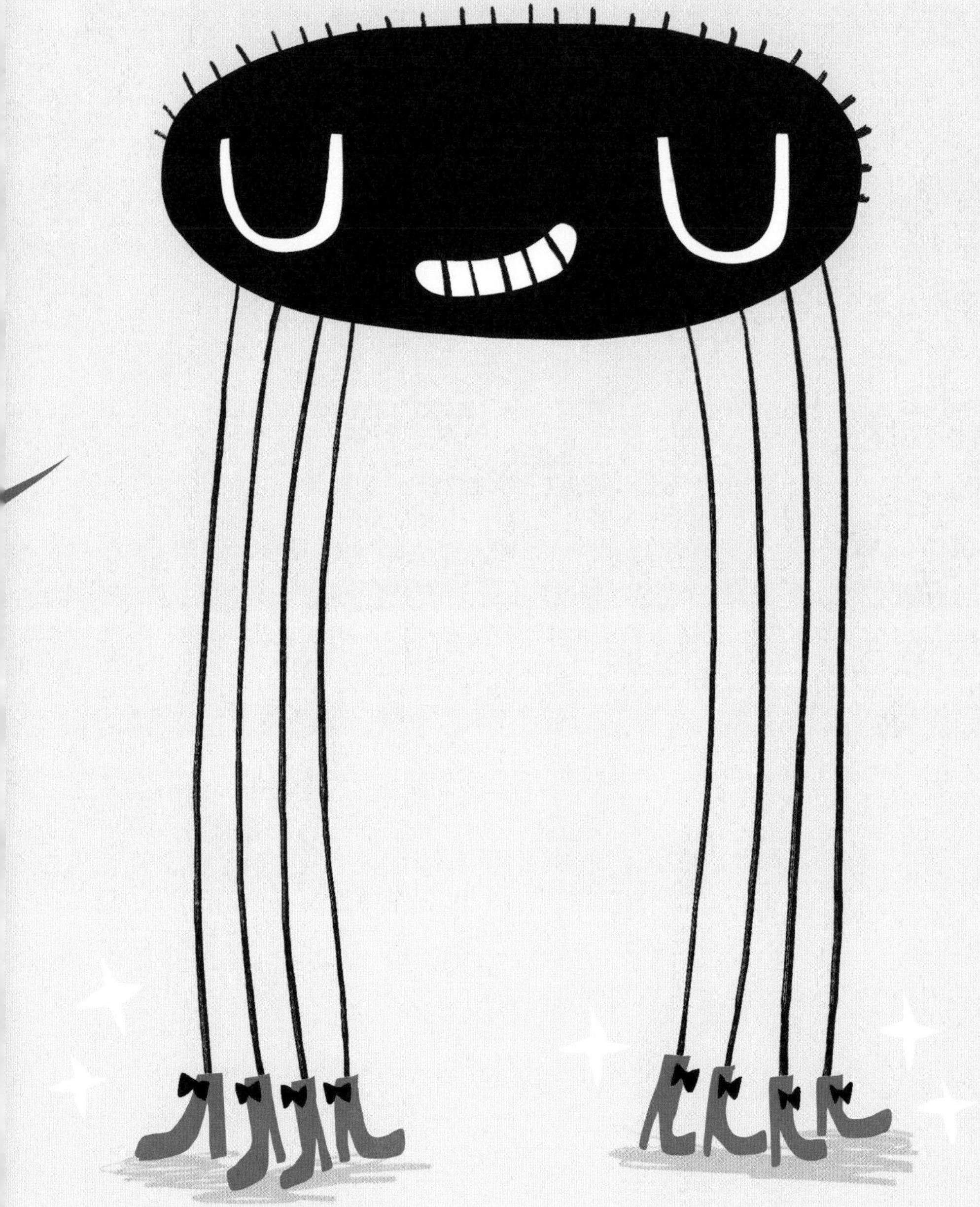

Most spiders have poisonous fangs in their mouths and

FOUR PAiRS OF EYES.

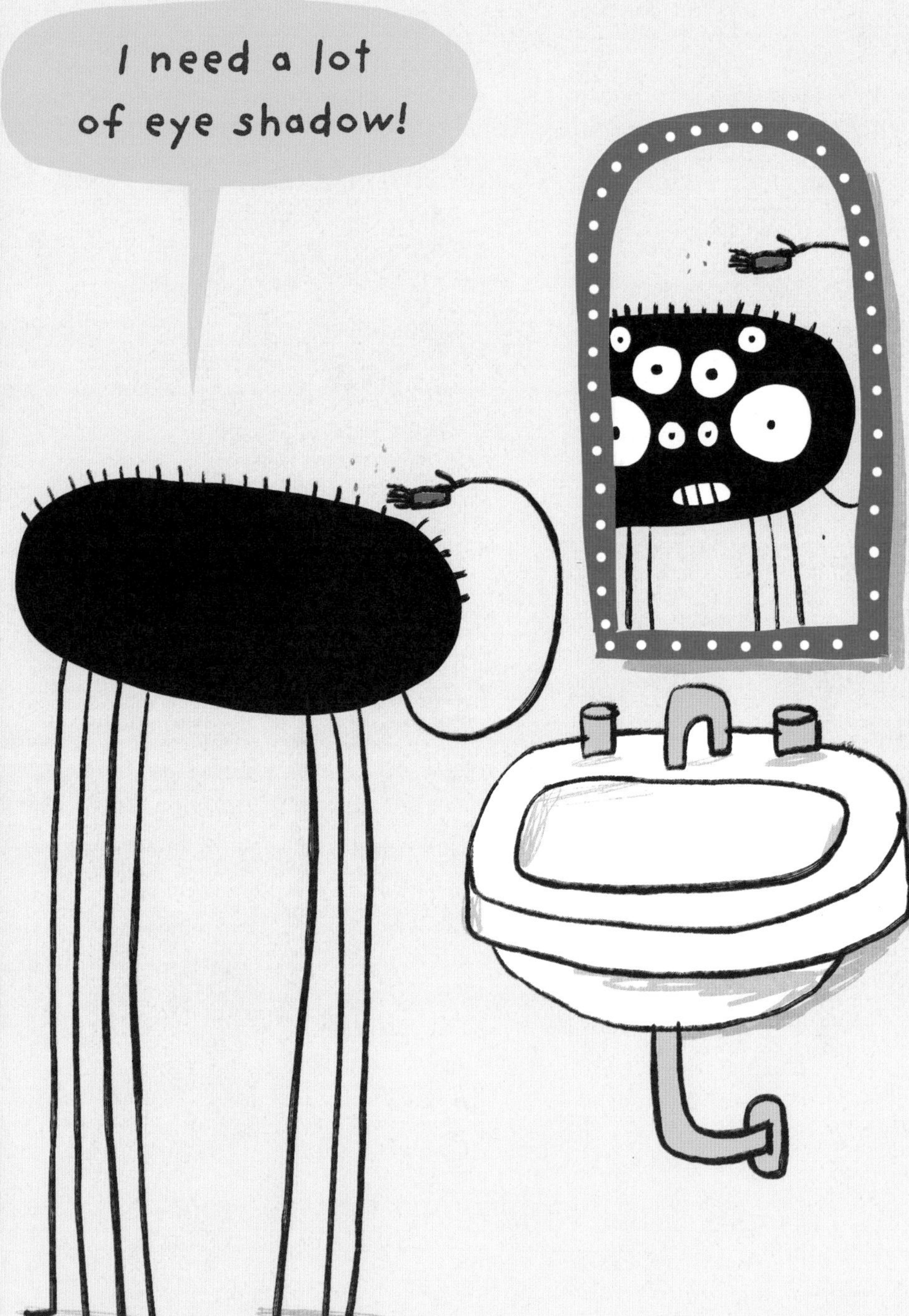
I need a lot of eye shadow!

Spiders produce

SiLK

with their abdomens.

Their silk can be used
for many things:

to build webs

oooYOYooo
OOOOOOO!

as a means of
transportation

to protect their eggs

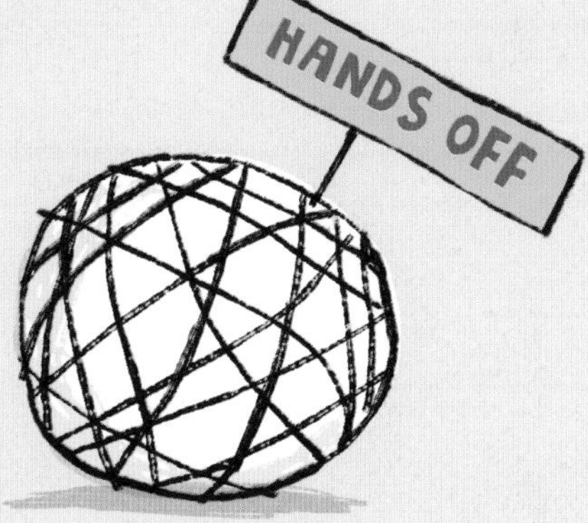
HANDS OFF

to create webs that
trap air so they can
breathe underwater.

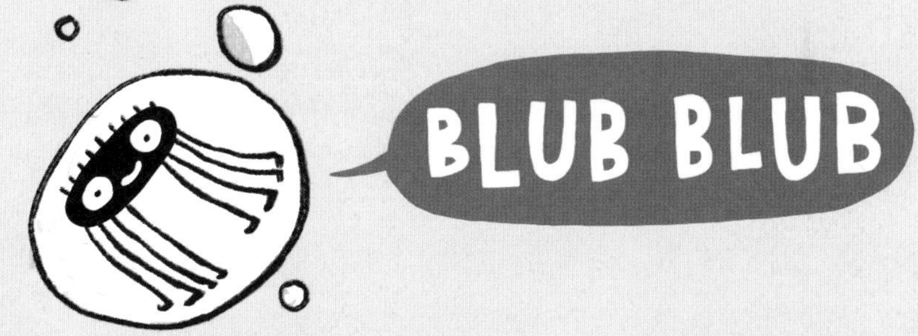
BLUB BLUB

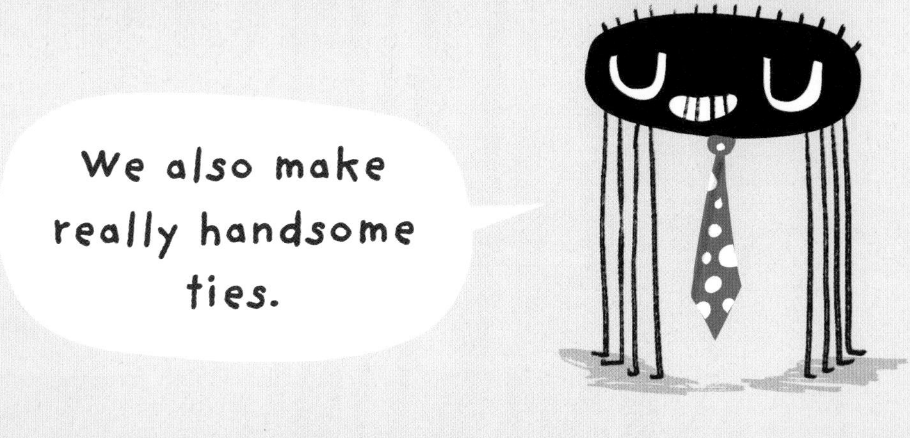
We also make really handsome ties.

Spiders mostly eat insects. They have many different ways of catching their prey: some use a sticky net as a trap, others jump on their prey and some catch their prey with a

LASSO.

YEEHAW!

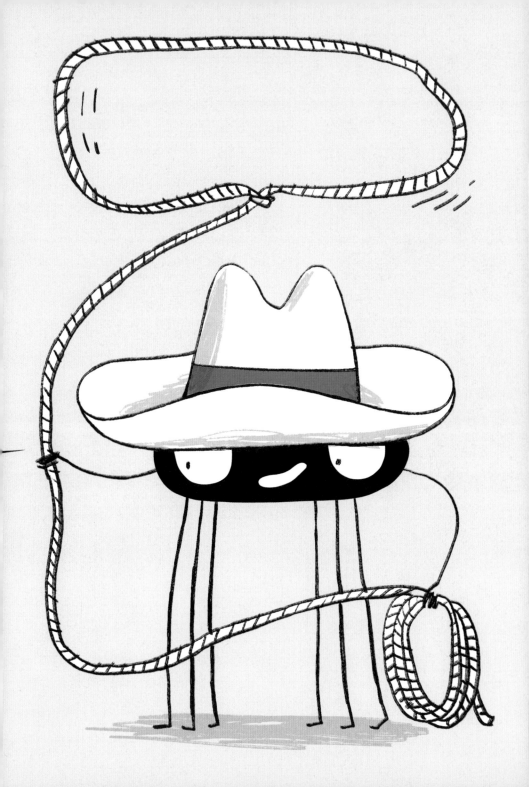

Some spiders even

MiMiC

their prey to make it easier to sneak up on them.

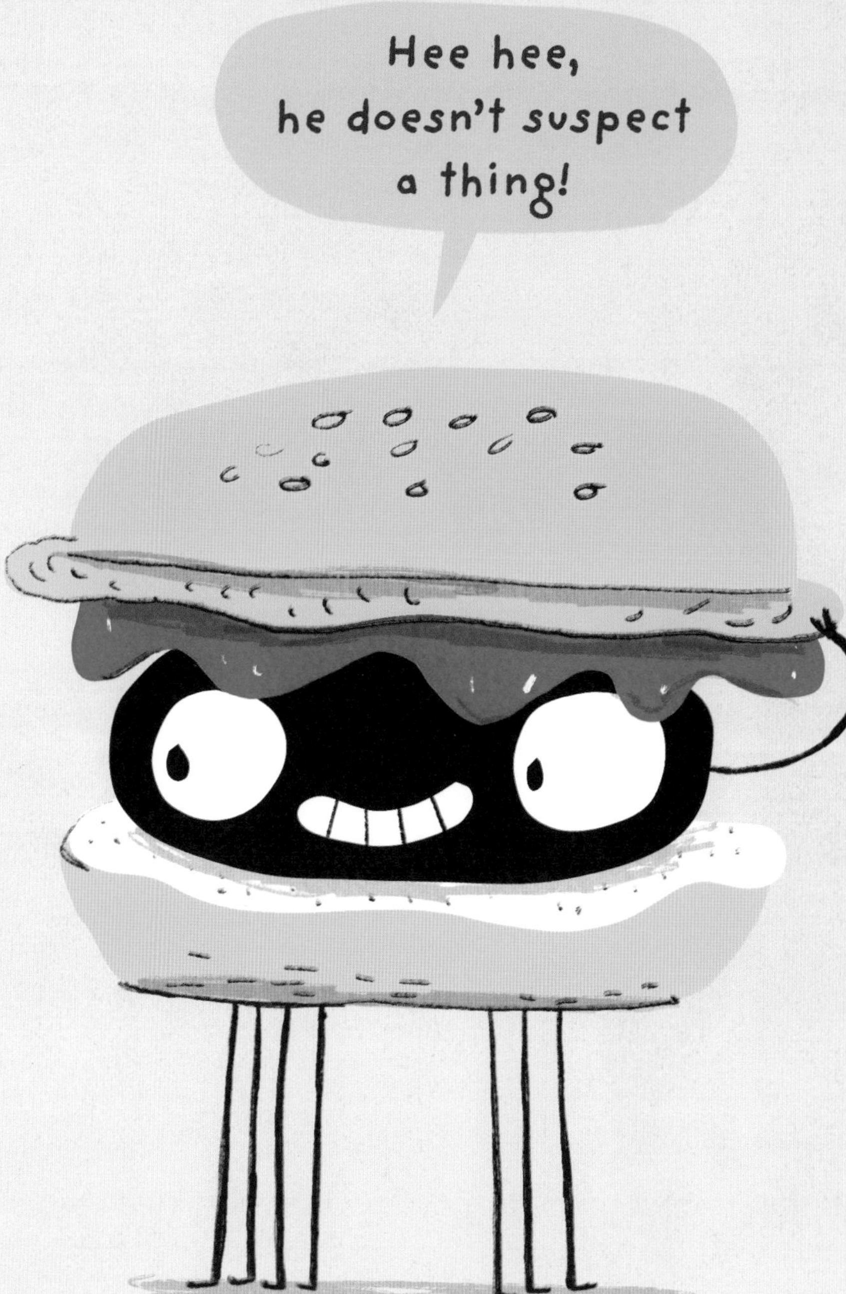
Hee hee,
he doesn't suspect
a thing!

In many spider species, the

FEMALE

is bigger than the

MALE.

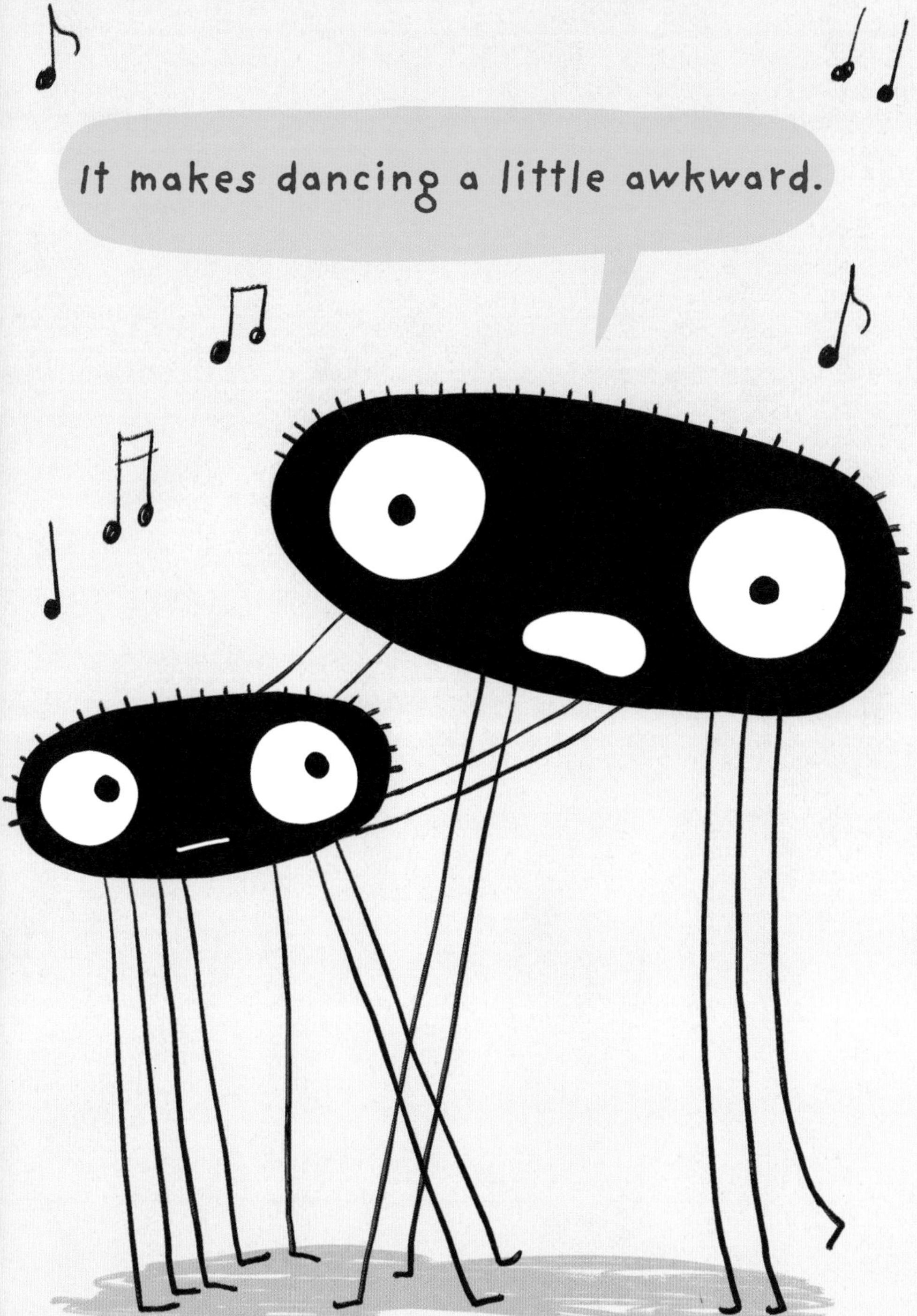
It makes dancing a little awkward.

After some spiders mate, the female spider will

EAT THE MALE.

GULP!

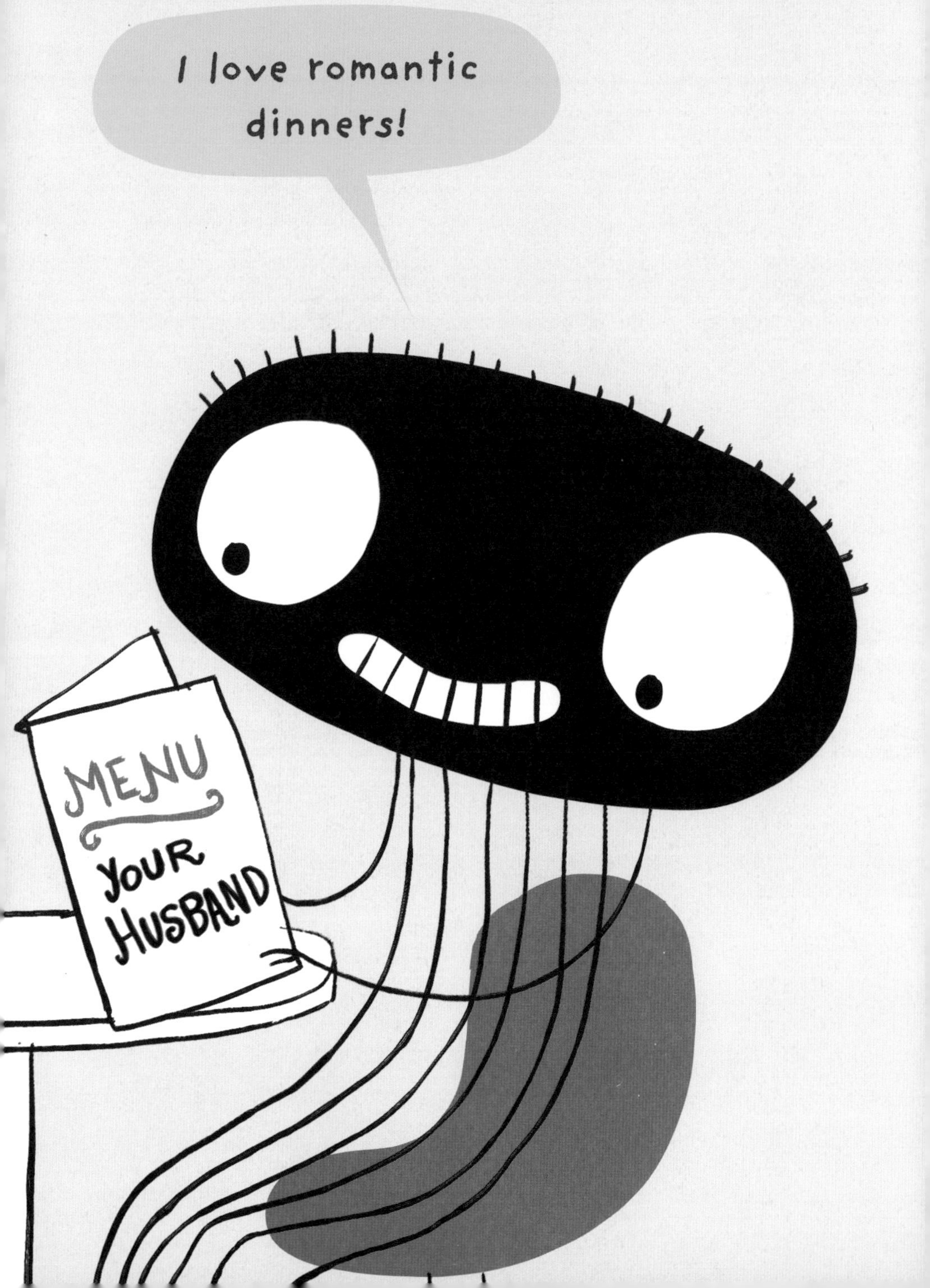
I love romantic dinners!
MENU
YOUR HUSBAND

The female spider can lay up to a thousand

EGGS.

She wraps them up in her silk and carries them around with her.

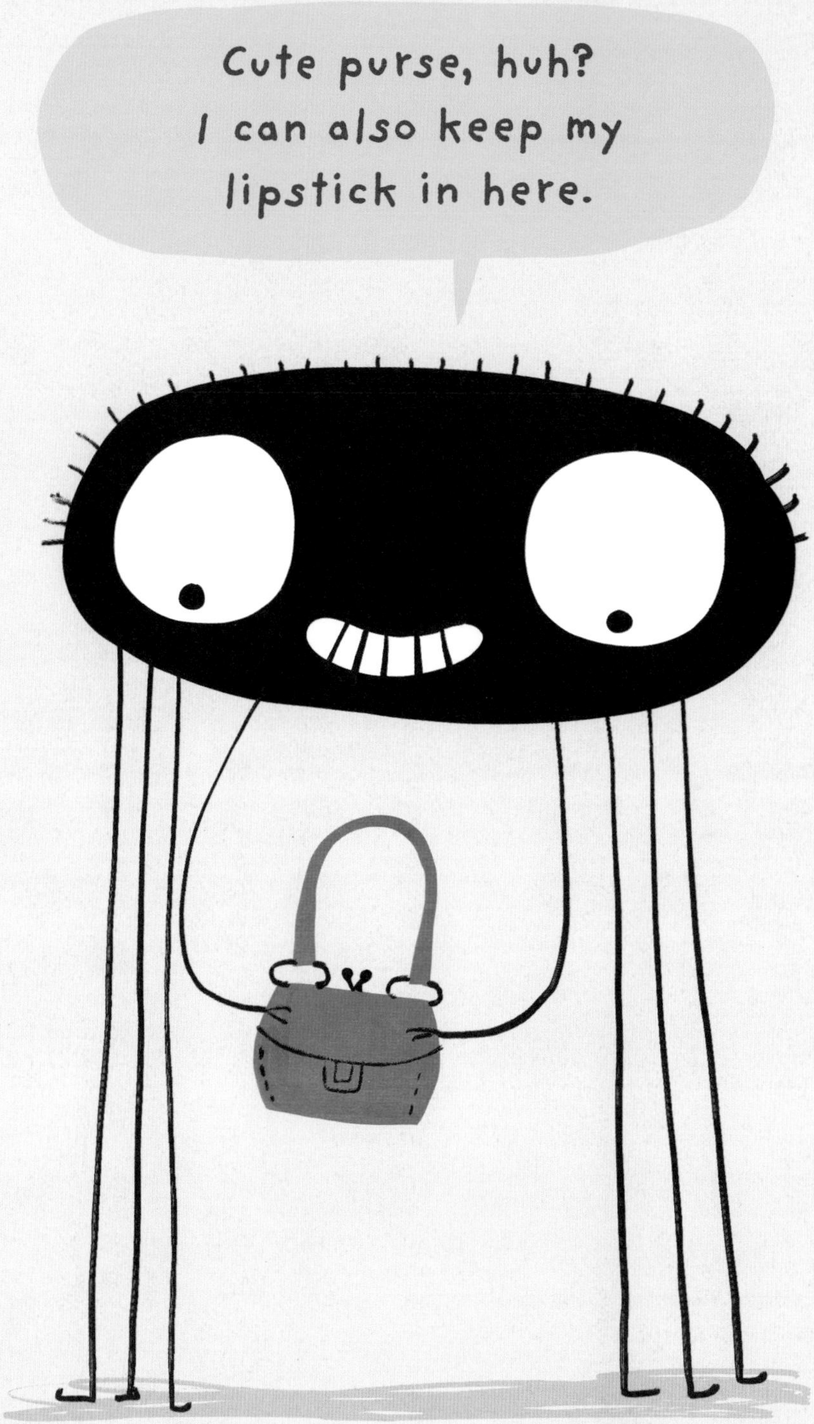
Cute purse, huh?
I can also keep my
lipstick in here.

Some mothers carry the baby spiders **ON THEIR BACKS** until the babies are old enough to **DEFEND** themselves.

Are we there yet?

Are we there yet?

Are we there yet?

People are often afraid of spiders,
but most spiders are

NOT DANGEROUS

to humans. In fact, spiders have much
more reason to be scared of us!

EEEEEEEEEK!

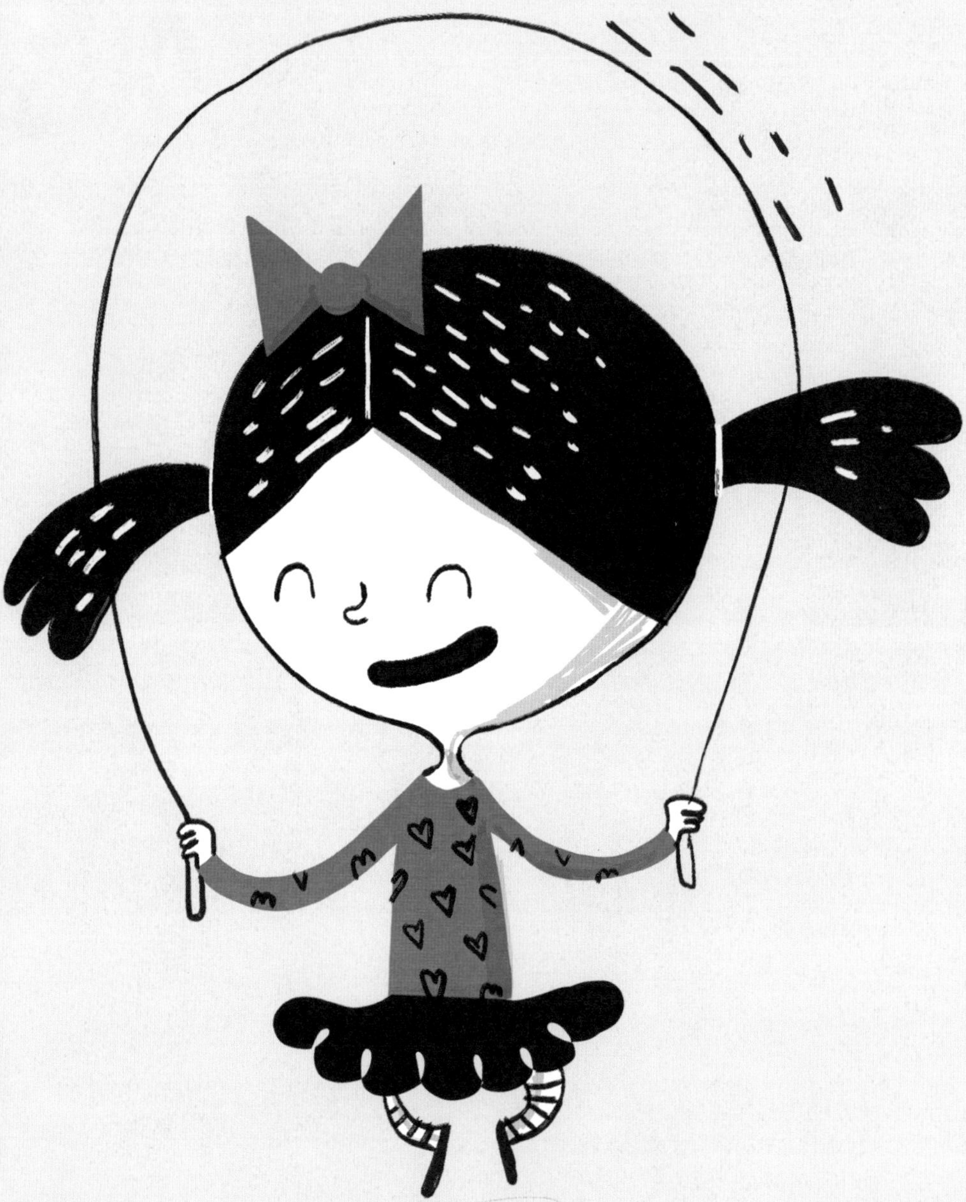

The spider can be helpful.
Since she eats

INSECTS,

she can get rid of annoying ones like mosquitoes and flies.

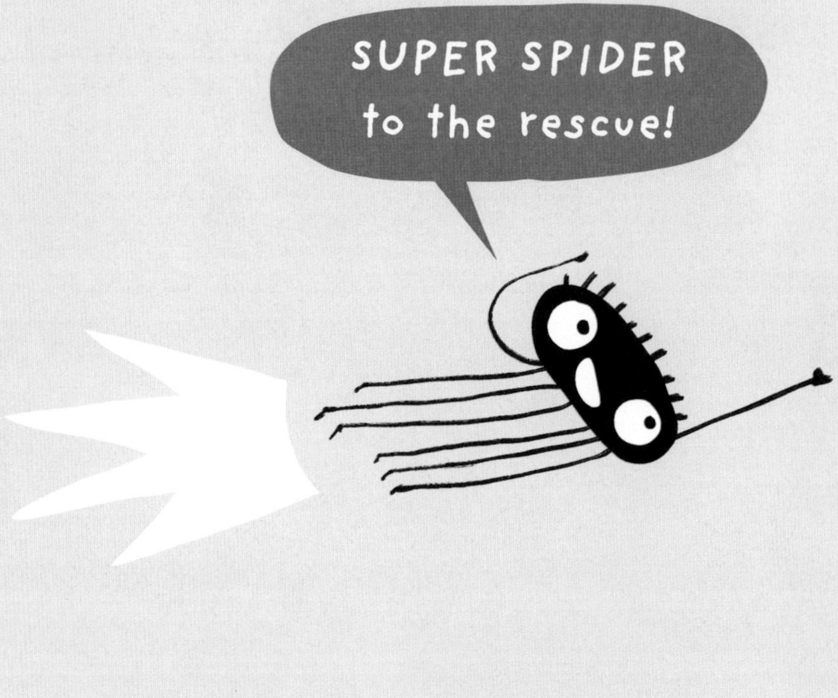
SUPER SPIDER
to the rescue!

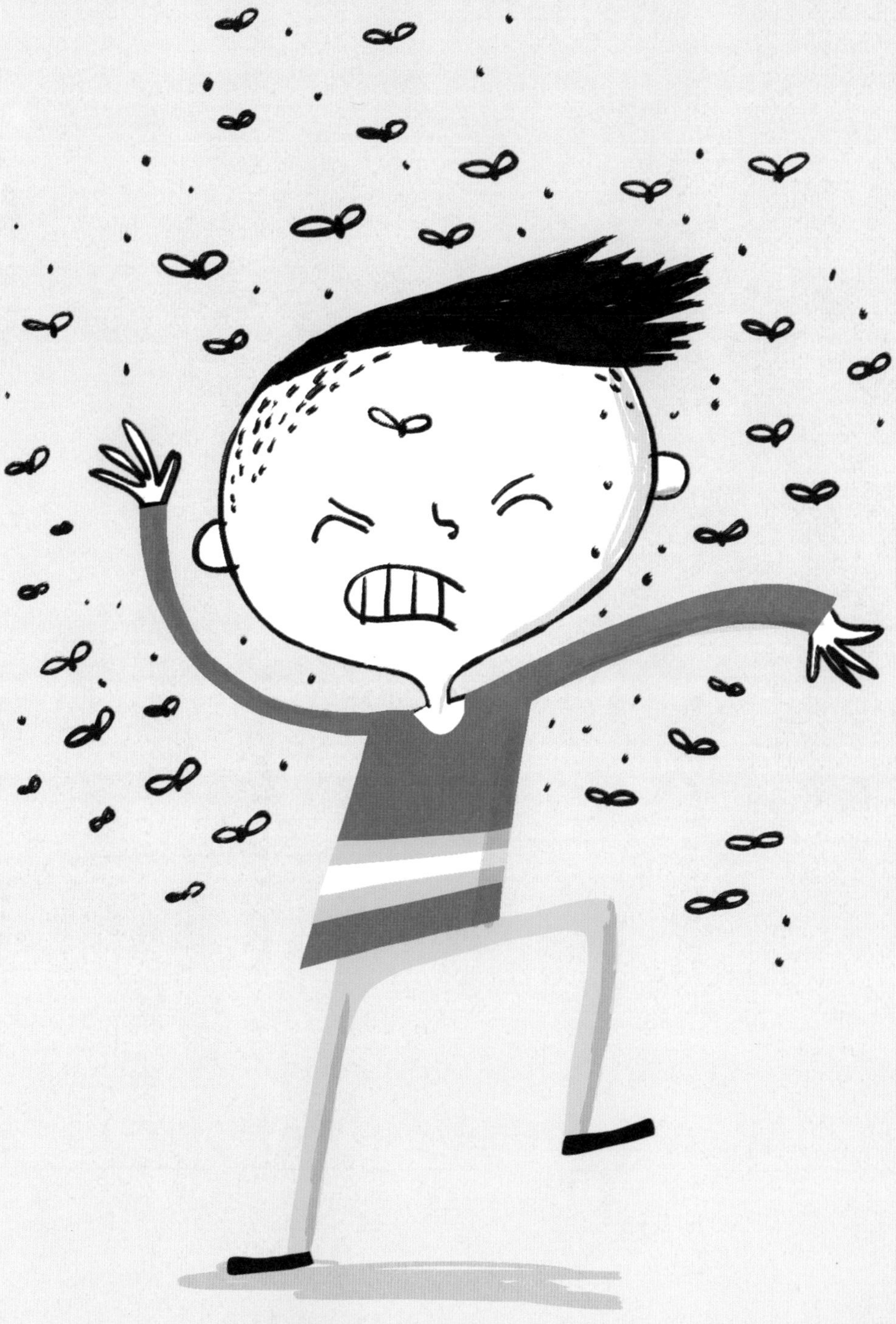

So the next time you meet a spider,
shake her

HAND!

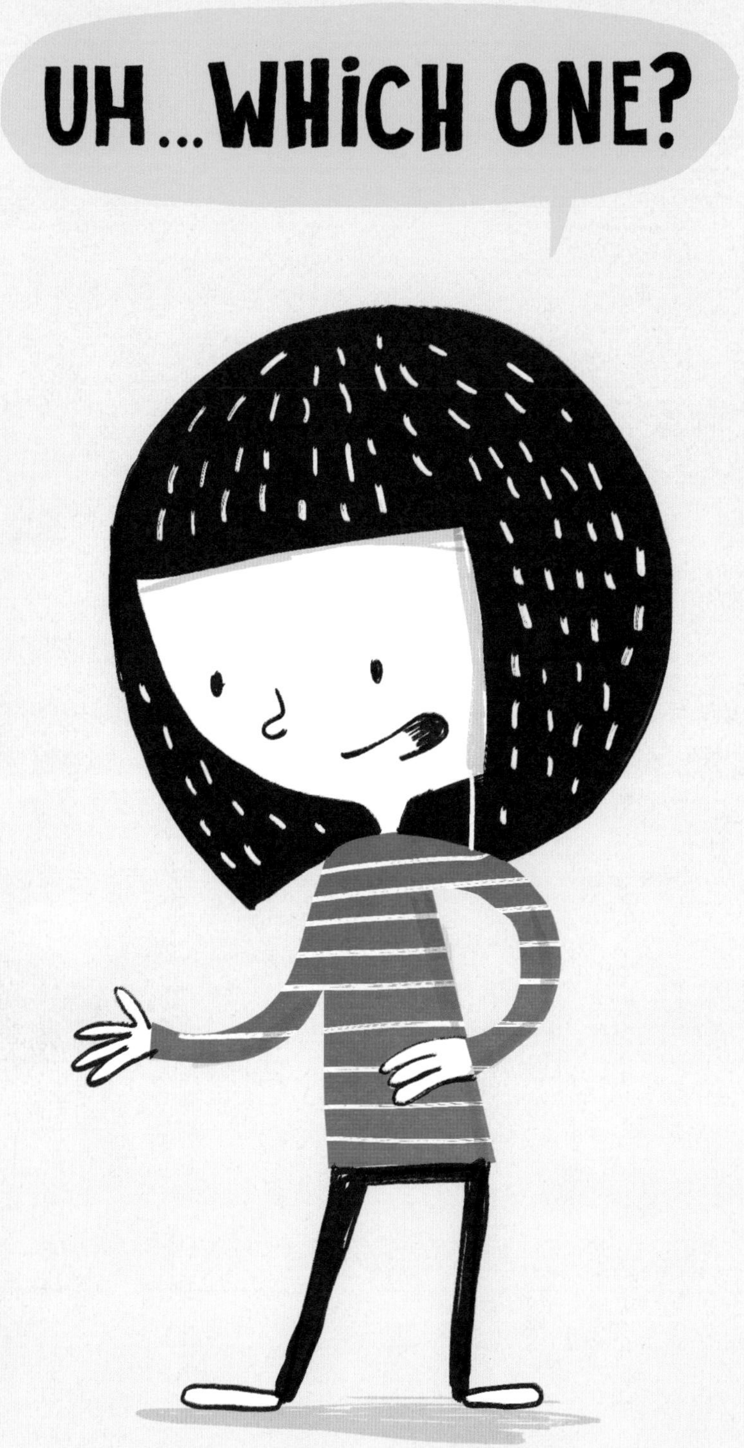
UH...WHICH ONE?

LOOK OUT FOR MORE

DISGUSTING CRITTERS

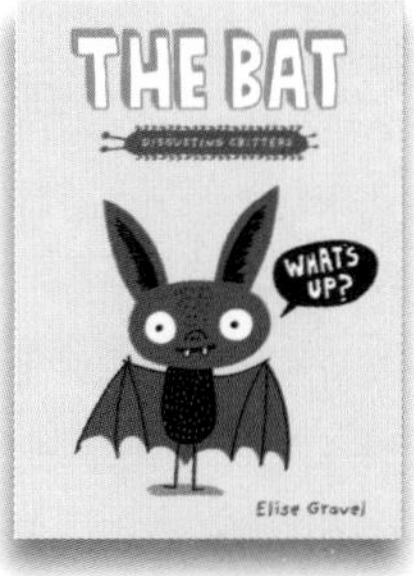
THE BAT
DISGUSTING CRITTERS
WHAT'S UP?
Elise Gravel

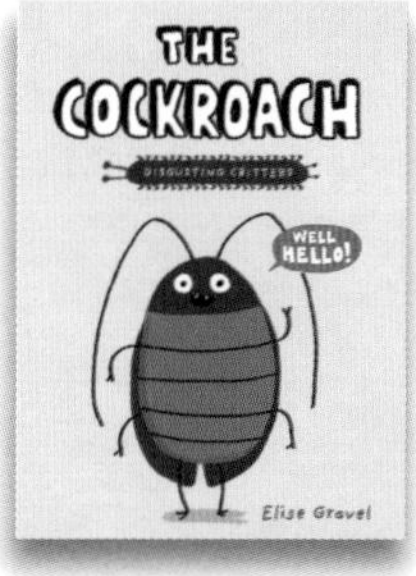
THE COCKROACH
DISGUSTING CRITTERS
WELL HELLO!
Elise Gravel

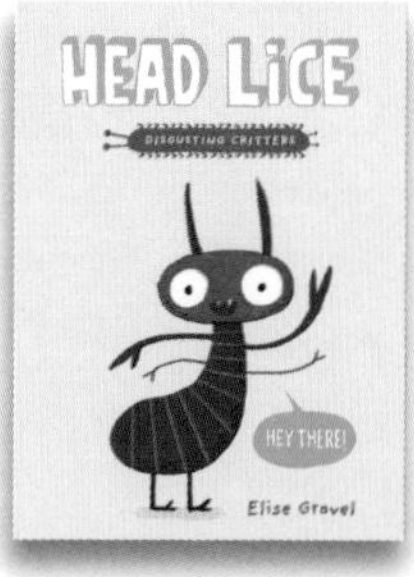
HEAD LICE
DISGUSTING CRITTERS
HEY THERE!
Elise Gravel

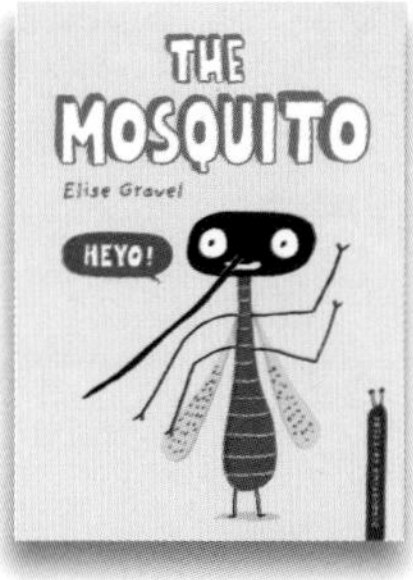
THE MOSQUITO
Elise Gravel
HEYO!

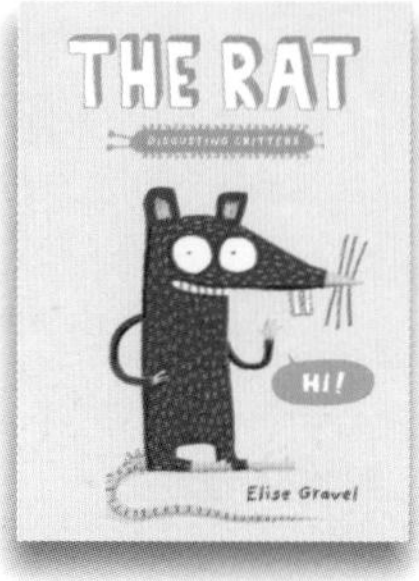
THE RAT
DISGUSTING CRITTERS
HI!
Elise Gravel

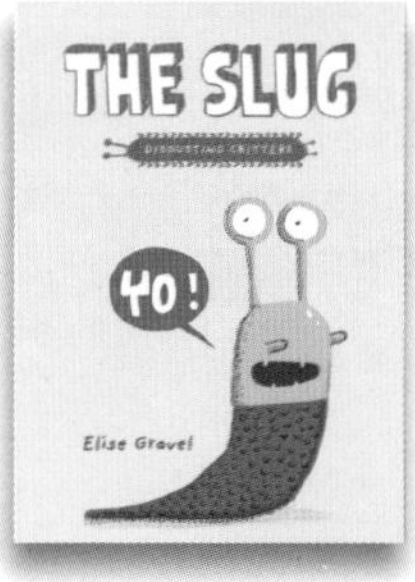
THE SLUG
DISGUSTING CRITTERS
YO!
Elise Gravel

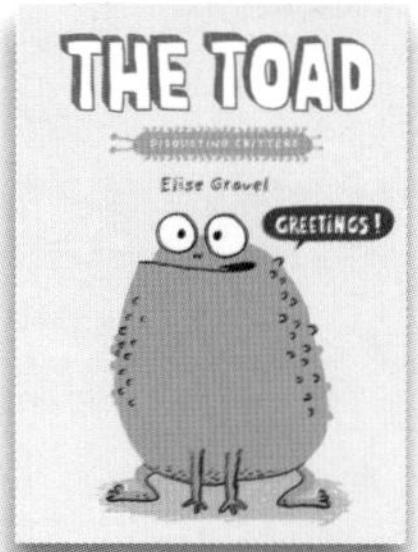
THE TOAD
DISGUSTING CRITTERS
Elise Gravel
GREETINGS!

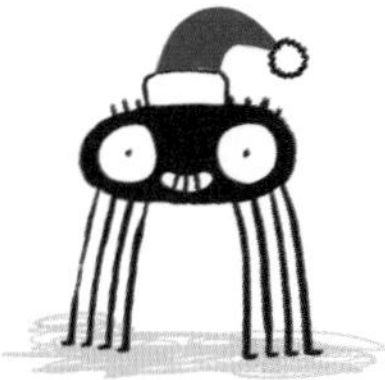